Sam Mnuguni Gloria Mnuguni Nomusa Buthelezi Sipho Mngomezulu Thandi
Gumede   Jerry Zisongo Phumzile Sibiya Fazira Magasela Phatwa MadloseFikile
Maxase Margaret Mdluli Sibongile Khumalo Virginia Qwabe Sipho Mathaba Lizan
Joubert Keshan Rambarum Samuel Mdluli Andries Khul..' ...za Grateful
Shozi Eunice Vilane   Florence Zulu Thandi ...   ... Prudence
Thabethe Gideon Nxunnalo Dumi Ndolou Gift...   ...ther Mnisi
Oscar Marimane Elneck Manyike Martha ...   ...e Karilina
Mabuza Figness Khosa Rene van Reenen Jonesta   ...uic Mkhabela Princess
Ngomane Philli Mkhatshwe Fikile Mhlabane Zodwa Sithole Annah Mbokodo
Patricia Ndaba Sibongile Nyundu Floris Smith Leanne Roberts Constance Mthabini
Eric Ubisi Vusi Mkhwanazi Florian Beaumann Lucien Beaumont Lettie Maila
Elmon Sithole Flora Nkuna Rally Khoza Stephalina Nyati Dudu Mandlhope
Christina Mabunda Virginia Mthabini Samson Mkhwanazi Bainame Ramadi
Pauline Tjetjoo Life Phalalo Gomolemo Fernando Constance Masasa Naledi Simon
Dineo Galesiiwe Teseletso Moitshoki Shadricky Kawana Filemon Khabeb Belinda
Kavendji Kabila Shanyengange Henry Langweni John Sitienei George Musembi
Joseph Nkoyo Pascal Wanyonyi Meshack Ondieki Owen Shivachi Michael
Lemiso James Nganga Salim Shaka Kazungu Lewa Evans Ondaria Michael
Chui James Kabisa Joseph Cheprion John Sayi   Simon Ondieki Richard
Agushoma Thomas Chagusia Masalu Kusenza Jackson Tumbago Kusekwa
Madigadi John Tumbago Paul Ndalo Sylidion Semazina Martin Doya Partice
George Upendo Beda Santiely Joseph Esther Justine Mashina Kaanankira
Leleiya Mbise Elias Ketuta Maison Lukene Witi ketuta Jackson Sepere Mwalimu
Ally Juma Mashaka Daniel Ndallu Salum Jumbe Kambi Lambi Rogers Michael
Max Raymond Harrison Msechu Gord Guido Mhalwike Mashaka Lukosi Fadhili
Kondo Yussuf Mkumbege Selemani Doga Hassan Kitimla Juma Lusonzo Makame
Kundi Abdullah Mbwana Jamal Samir Juma Salima Faki Denge Madodo
Foum Denge Mkadam Mati Mcha Denge Foum Hamis Kibabu Mwinga Mcha
Sheila Steenkamp Ashleigh Harris Anna Ridgwell Silwood Kitchen Trainees

A Kitchen Safari

Stories & Recipes From The African Wilderness

Yvonne Short

&BEYOND

Unsung heroes, tireless, passionate, talented: the men and women of &BEYOND kitchens are the modest magicians of mealtimes. In the bush, the heat can be fierce, and in the kitchens the temperatures often soar. But the show goes on: chopping, peeling, slicing, stirring, baking, flash-frying, sautéing, flambéing ... accompanied by melodic singing and good-natured bantering. Guests' children are welcomed into the kitchen with open arms, wrapped in voluminous aprons, topped with tiny chef's hats, hoisted onto chairs and included in the food preparations. African hospitality is nowhere more evident than in the kitchen.

Struik Lifestyle
(an imprint of Random House Struik (Pty) Ltd)
Company Reg. No. 1966/003153/07
80 McKenzie Street, Cape Town 8001
PO Box 1144, Cape Town, 8000, South Africa

www.randomstruik.co.za

First published in 2004 by Struik Publishers
Reprinted in 2005, 2006, 2007, 2008
Second edition published in 2009

Author: Yvonne Short
Copy editor: Shona Bagley
Designer: Hayley Jasven
Food by: Yvonne Short and Scott Rattray
Photographic credits: All photographs © Dook (www.dookphoto.com) with
the exceptions of those appearing on pages 2, 3, 17, 22, 31, 44, 53, 60,
71, 82, 83, 115, 116, 189, back flap of cover and back cover © &Beyond/
David Ballam

Publisher: Linda de Villiers
Printing and binding: Craft Print International Pte Ltd, Singapore

ISBN 978-1-77007-807-9

&BEYOND
www.andbeyond.com

www.imagesofafrica.co.za
IMAGES OF AFRICA
PHOTO LIBRARY

Contents

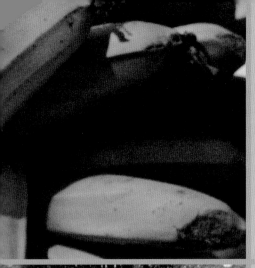

"The safari was unforgettable, the lodge was
first-class and the food was sublime.
I thought we may have to take one of the
chefs home with us!"

Lodge Guest Book

A Food Safari of the Soul

More than two decades ago there was a pioneering safari camp in the remote South African bushveld. It was founded with vision, passion, energy and little more than 12 rooms and a charcoal-fuelled fridge. Much behind-the-scenes sleight-of-hand ensured that guests at the camp were blissfully unaware of the shortage of tablecloths, the kitchen calamities and the vertiginous learning curve of chefs from the local communities, among their number poachers, refugees and farm labourers.

Local legend has it that in really lean times, unsuspecting guests were fed via the kitchen of a neighbouring lodge!

By the early 2000s, this humble safari camp had given rise to an internationally renowned ecotourism company, &BEYOND (formely CC Africa), which now owns 46 celebrated lodges and camps in six African countries. Following the success of our first camps and lodges in South Africa, the company embarked on a trans-African expansion programme in 1995, aiming to find the most desirable wilderness locations on the continent, build environmentally sound lodges, and deliver the consummate African guest experience which would also benefit the communities surrounding our lodges.

With this development phase came the desire to reflect, embody and celebrate the magnificent continent of Africa. We wanted the food cooked and served with love in our lodges to be an infusion of flavours from the Cape to Cairo, from Dakar to Zanzibar. Our desire was to unveil a mixed masala of tantalising tastes, of spicy, smoky, exotic aromas and flavours blending with the dramatic scenery of the wild African bush. We wanted to invoke the romance of eating al fresco around a candlelit table under a canopy of lantern-lit trees beneath a star-strewn African sky. We wished to deliver an experience to our guests that encapsulated the boundless hospitality and sensuality of Africa: An evocative odyssey that would awaken their senses – visual, tactile, textural, aromatic, aural and the sixth element … spiritual. Because &BEYOND believes in not only exceeding expectations in providing for the mind and body – our mission is to reawaken the souls of our guests.

And we believe that Africa, the mother continent, is the ultimate destination to deliver on these promises. Africa is a land of incredible diversity and almost inconceivable contrasts, with its colourful cultural splendours, its famine, its drought and internecine battles. Africa boasts some of the most exciting cuisine in the world, yet paradoxically and tragically, many who live here have so little. It is a continent of great contrasts: wild, exciting, sometimes bountiful, sometimes drought-stricken or flooded. Above all else, however, it is a beautiful, vital continent with the most wonderful climate, naturally hospitable people and an abundance of exotic, delicious and colourful produce.

We wanted our food to exude the essence of Africa's richness, its history and its soul. We were determined that our food would celebrate rather than corrupt the continent's fresh produce with Western fads and fussiness. The freshest of the fresh locally produced food was our aim, purchased from surrounding communities: lusty limes, fragrant vanilla pods, luminous lemon grass shoots, heady handfuls of mint, ruby-red tomatoes bursting with flavour and nourishment from the African sun. African food is wholesome and natural – not drowned in sauces and over-processed, over-reduced and over-presented.

We invite you to feast your senses on African's culinary glories.

Africa - A Smorgasbord for the Senses

&BEYOND food fundis set off in 1998 on a gastronomic journey of discovery. They felt that lodge food in South Africa was becoming too formulaic and predictable, featuring the ubiquitous buffet and *bain marie*. A search-and-research reconnaissance of Africa and its food inspired the Pan-African cuisine subsequently served in &BEYOND's lodges – the hallmark being the joy of cooking, feeding and sharing food. Their epicurean odyssey unearthed both authentic ingredients and local serving platters and vessels such as the tagines that characterise &BEYOND's tables. They also observed and absorbed the manner in which food was served from region to region – the rituals and customs that make mealtimes special.

Yvonne's and Nicky's two-week whirlwind circumnavigation of Africa commenced in West Africa – Côte d'Ivoire and Senegal and then on to Morocco. After a fleeting visit to Cairo, they travelled through Eritrea and Ethiopia, then to Kenya, Tanzania and Zanzibar before returning to South Africa.

West Africa

For countless centuries the tables of West Africans – from the great gold-trading Ashanti kings to the humble artisans – have groaned with tamarind, coconut, giant crabs, swordfish and hibiscus nectar. Like the tapestry of colour that typifies their markets, West African food is zesty, exciting and spontaneous. It is a celebration of precious bounty – huge bowls overflowing with deep-fried plantain chips or *fufu* (grated maize meal, manioc or cassava and very aptly named as it has a glue-like consistency that sticks to your fingers) wrapped in banana leaves, young coconuts, barbecued corn and newly peeled pineapples. The West African culture surrounding food springs from an abundance of fresh produce in a steamy 'promised land' of plenty, pressed up against the vast, thirsty Sahara Desert.

The cuisine is characterised by a curious blend of carefree enjoyment and frugal use of the produce at hand – every hollowed-out pumpkin shell is turned into a bowl, or carved and studded in the elaborate West African style and crafted into a musical instrument. Banana and Elephant Ear leaves are used in place of foil to wrap and steam maize and millet and then unfolded to become a plate.

In Cote d'Ivoire, one of the treasured dishes is palmnut soup with fufu. This substantial soup, based on the pulp of palmnuts, also includes lamb shanks, onions, tomatoes, chillies, giant crabs and sundried fish, with the fufu mounded in the middle of the dish like a large mountain. *Kejenou* is another favourite, invariably made with chicken and vegetables and traditionally cooked in an earthenware pot. This dish can also combine chicken, prawns, paprika, peanut oil, onions, garlic, tomatoes, chillies, cinnamon, nutmeg, saffron and rice.

Senegalese specialities include *Poulet* or *Poisson Yassa* – marinated and grilled chicken or fish blanketed in onions caramelised in lemon juice; *Mafe* which is a peanut-based stew; *Tieboudienne* – cabbage and fish stuffed with chilli, chunks of yam, whole okra and whole baby brinjal, served with very hot roasted baby red peppers on a pile of dirty rice. Steeped in the fundamental discipline of and quintessential reverence for Islam, Morocco is a completely different culinary experience in Africa. Just as every wall is tiled and carved in intricate Arabian patterns, Moroccan food is a lavish yet painstaking and deferential affair. Great respect and ceremony surrounds a fantasia of tastes and aromas with a backdrop of voluptuous orange trees bowing beneath cobalt-blue skies and the towering Atlas Mountains.

The ancient proverb goes "In Marrakesh you will eat with your eyes" and this holds true for the markets to this day. Moroccan cuisine has its roots in nomadic reverence for food and the wealth of the Saharan titans, and is characterised by exotic spices and laborious cooking methods. The market is an indulgence in pure visual excitement – picture the myriad heaped piles of aromatic spices, grains, legumes and fruits, including ruby red pomegranates, preserved lemons, *jujbes* (like a very small apple), prickly pears, glistening olives in every colour imaginable, and everywhere the hallowed Moroccan staple – the round flat bread.

Like all Africans, Moroccans are renowned for their hospitality – each guest is treated like royalty and their comfort and enjoyment is paramount. In the case of a *diffa,* or banquet, the host's hospitality is measured by course after course of sumptuous dishes in lavish quantities. Before the feast begins, a simple word from the host, *Bismillah*, invokes Allah's blessing. Hunks of warm bread are passed to the guests gathered around the opulent table as the first course begins – usually an assortment of exquisitely seasoned exotic salads.

Next comes the presentation of the *bastilla* – a dish of shredded fowl (pigeon or chicken) set in a custard infused with ginger, saffron, garlic and fresh coriander and wrapped in delicate layers of *ouarka* (similar to phyllo pastry). In between the petal-thin layers nestle sugar, ground almonds and cinnamon. A savoury tagine course follows – a luscious combination of meat, poultry, vegetables or fruit, simmered in sauces redolent with cumin, saffron and preserved lemon or honey. After the tagine is cleared away a mountain of steaming *couscous,* crowned with vegetables and baptised with broth, is set in the centre of the table and, once again, served with ceremony. Dessert would normally consist of fresh fruit pastries and mint tea made from Chinese gunpowder green tea and Moroccan mint.

North & East Africa

From North Africa, the food served in our lodges drew from Mediterranean influences – olives, oilseeds, chickpeas, dates, figs and pomegranates. The dishes reflect a dramatic history of centuries of diverse peoples and their civilisations. It is the place where Arabia, Africa and Europe merge, and the people, culture and cuisine are a heady and exotic blend. A lamb casserole with fresh dates cooked in sesame oil and infused with honey is reminiscent of Morocco. Early morning rusks made with honey, flavoured with cinnamon and drenched in sweet wine are served with fresh ice cold fruit and Turkish coffee, or a French-inspired omelette with freshly sautéed garlic and chopped fresh mint with an Arabian drink of chilled milk infused with almonds and orange makes for an exotic breakfast.

Ethiopia, Eritrea, Tanzania and Kenya were our next stops, where we discovered strong Arabic, English and German influences in East African cooking. The region produces coconuts, cashews, rice, maize, vegetables and an aromatic array of Zanzibari spices. From these regions in Africa we use pawpaws, peanut soups and deep-fried breads, sweet potato and pumpkin dumplings with goat's cheese and roasted macadamia nuts, spinach with coconut milk and peanut sauce, pumpkin tendrils and flowers in cream with banana chips – all adding deliciously different layers to our cuisine.

The pounding of wooden pestles in time-worn mortars, the grinding of aged stone against stone; the sizzle of meat over the coals of an open fire; the bubbling of a potjie - these were and still are the sounds of African cooking. Much has changed but much has remained the same. *Anon*

South Africa

South Africa was the final inspiration for the creation of Pan-African cuisine. The country represents unusual combinations of ethnic cuisines: African (Venda, Xhosa, San, Sotho, Ndebele, Zulu, Shangaan, Pedi) Portuguese, French, English, Dutch, German, Greek, Afrikaner, Indian (Hindu and Muslim), Malay, Italian, Jewish and Chinese. One of the most complex and exciting contributions to the art of cooking in Africa evolved in South Africa. The Dutch are historically very fond of their food, and founded the colony as a pantry for ships on the long route from Europe to the East. The Dutch also introduced slaves from Java, Sumatra, India, Indonesia and Madagascar – each bringing to South Africa their traditional ways of preparing food.

The fare that best typifies South African cooking is Cape-Dutch Malay – shortened to Cape Cuisine – whose foundations nod to ancient Greek and Roman civilisations. The Malays introduced the art of pickling and preserving, and also created wonderfully original dishes. These include *bobotie*: minced beef baked in a rich custard of eggs, lemon and curry; *bredies*: beef or lamb cooked slowly and gently – with tomatoes, onions, garlic, green ginger, cardamom, coriander and fennel seeds and a touch of sugar – until the meat falls off the bone; *sosaties*: (kebabs) marinated meat on a skewer cooked over the open fire; and *smoorvis* (smothered fish): a centuries-old method using ingredients as diverse as lobster, crab, mussels or even hard-boiled penguin eggs. The fish is salted and air-dried for preserving, then flaked into spicy rice with ginger, chillies, tomatoes, sultanas, potatoes and onions – it's delicious with whole-wheat bread and *atjar* (pickles).

Lamb with wild lavender is a recipe dating back to when the 1820 British Settlers introduced merino sheep to the Karoo – hardy livestock that feed on aromatic wild veld bushes and grow fat and tasty. A leg of lamb is cooked in buttermilk, lemon, garlic, cream, sherry and lavender. Unusual, completely delicious and another tormentor to the dieter.

Necessity, the canny mother of invention, guided early cooks and shaped their culinary skills. Food was foraged from the veld, or fished from sea and shore, and cooked over the embers of a fire. The art of *potjiekos* — the ultimate one-pot fare, developed in tandem with the open-grid *braai* (barbecue) which, with ice-cold beer characterises most sunny South African Sunday afternoons.

The most famous of all South African sweet treats are *koeksisters* and *melktert*. The worth of many a wife in the 1800s was measured by the quality of her *melktert.* In summer, pastry dough was made late at night then wrapped in a damp muslin cloth and hung in a draft to keep cool. For the lightest crust, the tart was baked before sunrise. The custard was flavoured with dried *naartji*e (tangerine) peel. Dusted with cinnamon, a *melktert* is an unusual taste sensation.

Indigenous food traditions live on, passed down from one generation to the next. Wild figs are eaten fresh or made into jam; wild Cape sorrel is simmered in soups and added to stews; pelargonium petals are used as herbs; various spinach-type plants (*marog*) are turned into pastes and pestos; *kinkelbossie* (twisted bush) are added to bredies; pumpkin leaves are cooked into a mush and eaten with pap; raw meat is salted, spiced and dried and eaten on bread, or added to vegetable stews.

And that was the conclusion to &BEYOND's epicurean journey of discovery on the African subcontinent. Many kilograms heavier, and laden with the myriad fruits of their pursuit, Yvonne and the team were also immeasurably enriched by their personal encounters with the wonderfully warm, hospitable and fascinating people of Africa.

We hope that this book, imbued with the love of Africa and its food, enchants you, too.

Training into Treasured Chefs

Guests often ask the question 'Where do you find all these talented chefs who feed us so well?' Training is a way of life for &BEYONDers – constantly learning, upskilling and sharing knowledge is a core value of the company. Yet often the trainers themselves end up learning the most, and training workshops are always characterised by much laughter and cultural exchanges. That is the beauty and the reward of training in Africa. The theoretical components of &BEYOND's food workshops are generally held outdoors: in the dappled shade of a giant umbrella thorn, beneath the underwater-like canopy of yellow fever trees or surrounded by African savanna, with the call of the wild all around.

Due to construction delays, training sometimes occurs at the eleventh hour: with a lodge opening mere days away, a trainer can be seen in a dry riverbed, conducting intensive lessons with raw recruits from neighbouring communities. It's rigorous, and the results are often hair-raisingly hilarious. On the opening night of a brand-new lodge in South Africa, the trainers had to bite their lips while dignitaries were served dinner: one of the butlers, who days before had been a casual farm labourer, had placed neat squares of w.c tissue next to each plate. His trainer, noticing him carrying green napkins to the tables, had stressed that white napkins should be used. Being unable to find any in the kitchen storerooms, he decided to improvise. Meanwhile, another butler was asking a guest whether she'd like a red glass of wine, and a third, clearing plates from the tables during speeches, was unsure of what to do with them, so simply stacked them in towering piles on the floor in the dining room.

Lodge openings are not usually speckled with slapstick, but chef training is always a joyful affair. Over the years &BEYOND has sometimes 'inherited' a property, along with non-culturally aligned cuisine. Many established East African camps, for instance, still serve colonial-era cuisine, complete with mushroom soup starters and fussy French main courses and unsuitably heavy desserts. With proverbial new brooms, culinary cobwebs are swept out of the kitchens. It is sometimes difficult to teach old chefs new tricks, but step-by-step the real Africa is introduced into our camps and kitchens. Fresh, home-grown ingredients used in the villages find their way into the food, *souferias* and *jikkos* no longer languish on stove tops – brought out into the light, buffed into burnished glory, they take pride of place in &BEYOND's bomas and on bush banquets. The logistics of getting certain food supplies to some of our very remote lodges are extraordinary, but everybody involved takes part enthusiastically, out of sheer love of feeding our guests delightful, unpretentious soul-food.

Cate Davis, one of &BEYOND's Chef Trainers, recounts: 'We train and train and train, and the more we train the more we, too, learn. We teach our trainees about delighting in exceeding guests' expectations. We in turn learn about customary, unquestioned African hospitality. We teach how to assemble the ultimate game-drive sundowner snack box, the most stylish "surprise" hamper, the perfect private deck dinner. We learn about the joy and vibrancy that characterise behind-the-scenes in an African kitchen – hips swaying to rhythmic beats, melodic voices joined in cyclical African songs, spices and laughter mingling to create an atmosphere undreamed of in an formal, Michelin-starred kitchen. We teach our chefs about our well-travelled, privileged, gourmet guests. They show us how to turn problems into solutions the African way – an unhurried, genuine empathy and a simple yet profound philosophy and approach to life.

'We learn humility as we tour a vegetable garden proudly owned and tended by some of our chefs in East Africa (they sell their vegetables to the lodge as one of the projects in &BEYOND's ongoing community empowerment initiatives). We are deeply moved by the evident pride which Mr Mugambe, the chief vegetable gardener, takes in his fresh ginger, lemongrass, mint, aubergines, beans, bananas and marrows. And we shake with laughter as he tells his tales of protecting his precious produce from the African wildlife pressing in. "Vegetable askaris" (security guards) are employed to ensure that baboons don't run off with the profits, and one memorable night, a brave askari kept a herd of 200 elephants at bay with a pot and ladle!

'We teach about kitchen equipment, fridge temperatures, storage, special dietary requirements, menu planning, knife skills, grilling, basting, sautéing, hygiene, children's menus, the corporate principles of &BEYOND, how to put the "wow!" into service and everything including the kitchen sink. We learn about the simple joy of service, of African hospitality, of "happiness" food made with love and served by real people.'

'We can plant a &BEYOND food culture in any soil that can grow a rose and still have the best result out of it no matter what, as long as we have given ourselves full commitment on it and understanding what the company is trying to achieve. In doing so, we'll always have happy returning guests who will spread the good news all over the world.'

May Kobero, Grumeti
Tanzania

Food is an adventure of sensuality -
the slipperiness of roasted peppers in olive
oil; the sensational melting of clotted
cream on warm cinnamon toast;
the velvet sexiness of the skin and the
pinkly moist inside of a fresh ripe fig;
the explosion of fragrance from a jar of
spice; the intense copper of saffron,
the machismo of cumin;
the fey fragility of almonds;
the sharpness of ginger
which crystallises into sweet
'take me I'm yours' sticky crispness
and the ultimate conqueror:
swashbuckling, take-no-prisoners garlic.

Cate Davis is our exceptional nomadic,
life-in-a-backpack chef trainer in
East Africa. Constantly on the move
between lodges and camps, she's a tall,
trim and tireless mentor.
Her wry sense of humour and patient
professionalism has inspired the
most junior kitchen staff to aspire
to be head chefs of whom
she could be very proud.

'There was a crashing of metal and wood on brick as guests skidded, threw glasses, grabbed loved ones, somehow managed to find time to down drinks and then fled to the safety of the reception area from whence they peered at the scene unfolding at Ngala's swimming pool. Five hundred buffalo emerged at high speed from the dry river opposite the pool. There was water to be had, and clean water at that. The parched bovids bustled up to the pool where they stopped, looking confused. Some tried to drink but it became apparent that the surface of the water was too far below the lip of the paving. One of the old bulls had obviously been studying humans frolicking at the pool for some time. He marched on through the herd and without missing a beat, dived in. Actually, "dive" implies grace, which a 700kg buffalo is noticeably short on. He drank, swam up and down once or twice and then, as if he had been engaging in this sort of thing for years, propelled himself to the shallow end where he emerged by means of the steps. We fully expected him to grab a towel and lie down under an umbrella. Instead he walked back to his herd with the superior air of someone who has achieved what most only dream of.'

&BEYOND
South Africa

Ngala Private Game Reserve, Mpumalanga

Phinda Private Game Reserve, KwaZulu-Natal

Kirkman's Kamp, Sabi Sand Game Reserve, Mpumalanga

Dulini Lodge, Sabi Sand Game Reserve, Mpumalanga

Exeter River Lodge, Sabi Sand Game Reserve, Mpumalanga

Leadwood Lodge, Sabi Sand Game Reserve, Mpumalanga

Madikwe Safari Lodge, North West Province

Kwandwe Private Game Reserve, Eastern Cape

African food is the last great culinary
frontier left in the world. The highest
mountains have been conquered,
the great rivers have all been explored
and named, vanished cultures have all
been resurrected, the Great Divides have
been spanned and bungee jumped.
Is there anything new under the sun?
Yes, this great new discovery on an
ancient continent:
Pan-African cuisine: new, intriguing
combinations and glorious flavours to woo
the most discerning of palates,
the greatest gourmand.

Pumpkin Soup Every Which Way

A firm favourite at every BEYOND lodge!
Each has its own unique way of
preparing this comfort soup.
Start with pumpkin, peeled and cubed and
simmered until soft in a good chicken stock
with leeks and a couple of potatoes.
Purée, season and serve hot or cold.
For fun, add any or a combination of the
following: apples, pears, orange zest
and juice, ground cinnamon, ground cumin,
ground coriander, touch of chilli,
fresh ginger, splash of balsamic vinegar.

Turkey with Pine Nuts and Sultanas

160ml sultanas

80ml pine nuts

5ml ground turmeric

10ml paprika

5ml ground coriander

10ml ground cinnamon

30ml mint leaves – chopped

30ml parsley – chopped

* Soak the sultanas in warm water to cover for 15 minutes and drain
* Toast the pine nuts until lightly golden in a dry frying pan
* In a large bowl, thoroughly combine sultanas, pine nuts, turmeric, paprika, coriander, cinnamon, mint, parsley, olive oil, lime juice and chillies
* Place turkey steaks in a ceramic dish, pour over mixture and marinate at room temperature for 2 hours, turning once
* Remove turkey from the marinade, brushing off any nuts or fruits
* Pour oil from marinade into a large frying pan and heat till quite hot
* Seal turkey steaks for 1 minute on each side until lightly golden. Add the marinade and cook for further 2 minutes or until turkey is done
* Place turkey steaks on serving dish and spoon remaining sauce on top
* Finish with segments of fresh orange and scatter with coriander leaves

Serves 4

125ml olive oil

2 limes – squeezed

2 red chillies – diced

4 x 150g turkey steaks – flattened

1 orange – segmented

1 small bunch fresh coriander – rinsed

Syrup:
1kg sugar
1.5 litres water
500ml orange juice
80ml lemon juice
2 oranges – zest only
5ml cream of tartar
2 cinnamon sticks
Dough:
750ml cake flour – sifted
15ml cornflour
15ml baking powder
pinch of salt

15ml butter
2 eggs
375ml milk
500ml vegetable oil
To serve:
250g halva – broken into pieces
250g dates – halved and
stones removed
Candied Lemon (optional:
see recipe page 32)

Koeksisters with Dates and Halva

To prepare the syrup:
✳ Dissolve the sugar in the water in a pan before it comes to the boil
✳ Bring to the boil, add orange juice and cook briskly for 15 minutes
✳ Allow to cool and add lemon juice, orange zest, cream of tartar and cinnamon sticks.
✳ Refrigerate overnight

To prepare the dough:
✳ In a large bowl, mix cake flour, cornflour, baking powder and salt
✳ Rub in butter
✳ Beat eggs and milk together and add to dry ingredients
✳ Knead for 12 minutes. Form into a ball, wrap in waxed paper and chill overnight
✳ Roll out to 10mm thickness. Cut into strips 3cm x 8cm. Starting 2cm from one end, cut each strip into 3, leaving all attached at one end. Plait together and pinch to seal
✳ Heat oil in a deep pan and fry koeksisters until golden brown – about 2–3 minutes
✳ Drain briefly on paper towel and plunge into cold syrup. Drain on a rack

To serve:
✳ Pile koeksisters on a large platter and scatter with halva, dates and candied lemon

We have been granted everything we've asked for and more. The hospitality was brilliant - accommodation - everything you need, the food - excellent. I did ask the chef's name tonight but have forgotten - courtesy of great wine and great company! He's provided us with gorgeous food at every meal and we have gained several blissful kilos!

4 lemons

1 vanilla bean – split

750ml sugar

2 litres water

Candied Lemon with Vanilla

✴ Score lemons from top to bottom and remove whole lengths of peel and pith
✴ Blanch in boiling water for 1 minute and drain
✴ Place vanilla, sugar and water in a large saucepan and boil over low heat
until sugar dissolves
✴ Add lemons and bring back to the boil
✴ Cook slowly till lemon is soft and syrup thickens and is clear in colour.
✴ Store in sterilised glass jars
✴ Serve with vanilla ice-cream, poached fruits and fruit tarts

Tomato, Tamarind and Ginger Soup

* Roughly break up the tamarind pulp with your hands and place in a mixing bowl
* Cover with 450ml warm water and leave to soak for 10 minutes
* Strain the mixture through a fine sieve into a small bowl, pushing the pulp through the sieve with the back of a spoon
* Discard the stones and fibres and set the tamarind liquid aside
* Place the tomatoes, garlic and ginger in a blender and process for 1 minute or until smooth and combined
* In a large saucepan, heat the tamarind liquid over a medium heat for 5 minutes
* Add the fresh coriander, green chilli, turmeric, black pepper and blended tomato mixture
* Bring the soup to a simmer for 15 minutes, stirring occasionally, being careful not to let the mixture boil
* Add salt to taste
* Heat the oil in a frying pan. Add the mustard seeds and, as they begin to pop, add the red chillies, cumin, coriander, curry leaves and asafoetida
* Fry for 1 minute, then remove from heat
* Pour the oil and spices over the soup and stir through
* Serve hot, garnished with fresh coriander

Serves 4

100g tamarind pulp
10 tomatoes – peeled and chopped
4 cloves garlic – peeled
2.5cm fresh root ginger –
peeled and finely sliced
small bunch of coriander –
finely chopped,
plus a few leaves for garnish
1 fresh green chilli – split lengthways
5ml turmeric

2.5ml ground black pepper
salt to taste
45ml vegetable oil
5ml mustard seeds
3 dried red chillies
2ml cumin seeds
2ml ground coriander
few curry leaves
small pinch of asafoetida

&BEYOND
Ngala Private Game Reserve

Ngala Safari Lodge & Ngala Tented camp

First private game reserve to be incorporated into the two million-hectare Kruger National Park

✳

Timeless cooking with a soupçon of sass

✳

Gorgeous Tented Safari Camp and exhilarating Walking Safaris

✳

Dazzling and prolific array of spectacular wildlife – one of South Africa's best-kept game-viewing secrets

✳

Member of Small Luxury Hotels Of The World

✳

Huge breeding herds of elephants

✳

Archbishop Desmond and Mrs Leah Tutu became patrons of Africa Foundation (founded by &BEYOND, now a non-profit community empowerment organisation) as a result of a visit to Ngala Private Game Reserve

African Roast Rib of Beef with Cumin

Roasted Beef:

1x4kg rib of beef — on the bone

45ml cumin seeds

45ml sea salt

Roasted Beetroot:

2kg beetroot – small to medium sized

15ml caraway seeds

10ml vegetable oil

125ml sherry vinegar

5ml brown sugar

Roasted beef:

✳ Allow the beef to stand, covered at room temperature for two hours before cooking

✳ Preheat oven to 220°C

✳ Rub beef all over with the cumin, and a generous amount of salt

✳ Place meat bone side down on roasting tray and place in oven. Roast at 220°C for 10 minutes

✳ Turn oven down to 160°C and start timing: 2h20 for medium rare; 2h40 for medium; 3h for well done

✳ Once beef is cooked to your liking, remove from oven and allow to rest in a warm place for at least 20 minutes

✳ Serve with Roasted Beetroot

Roasted Beetroot:

✳ Wash beetroot and trim, leaving 5cm of stalk. Place in boiling salted water and cook until almost done

✳ Drain, cool and roll skins off with fingers

✳ Toss with caraway seeds, oil, sherry vinegar and brown sugar

✳ Place in roasting tray and roast in a preheated 180°C oven for 20 minutes (while beef is resting)

✳ Serve with pan juices

Serves 12

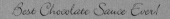

Best Chocolate Sauce Ever!

Melt 80g butter, add 50g sifted cocoa powder and cook gently for a couple of minutes. Add 140g tin of evaporated milk and 200g icing sugar and bring to the boil, stirring continuously. Cook for five minutes.

So good you'll not want to share it with anyone!

Elmon Dumi has achieved so much, taught so many and inspired an entire company. He started as a waiter and is now the Executive Chef at Ngala. Constantly churning out well-trained chefs and yummy food, Dumi is chief among our treasured chefs.

41

8 roma or plum tomatoes

5ml sea salt

5ml sugar

5ml ground black pepper

10ml fresh thyme leaves – chopped

10 ml olive oil

15ml fresh oregano leaves – chopped

300g soft goat's cheese

1 small jar vine leaves in brine,
washed well to remove salt

To serve:

fresh salad leaves

vinaigrette

black olives - pitted

caper berries

Baked Goat's Cheese in Vine Leaves with Roasted Tomatoes, Olives and Capers

✳ Split tomatoes lengthways and place cut side up on roasting tray.Sprinkle over the sea salt, sugar, black pepper and thyme and drizzle with olive oil

✳ Bake in a preheated 160°C oven for 20 – 25 minutes, till lightly browned and soft. Set aside

✳ Mix together the oregano and goat's cheese

✳ Shape into 4 'cakes' about $1\frac{1}{2}$ cm high

✳ Rub a little olive oil onto the vine leaves and, using 2 per cheese, carefully wrap up the filling

✳ Place in a preheated 180°C oven and bake for 10 minutes until the leaves are well coloured and the filling hot

To serve:

✳ Place goat's cheese parcels alongside the roast tomatoes

✳ Finish with some fresh salad leaves tossed in vinaigrette, black olives and caper berries

✳ Serve immediately

Serves 4

Gift Khoza, who is from the Hluvukani
community neighbouring Ngala, began
her career as a buffet attendant at
Ngala in 1994. Moving through
the ranks to junior then senior chef,
she is now the assistant head chef.
With her characteristic beaming smile,
Gift says 'I am very proud to be working
for &BEYOND. Through all the
training I have learned a lot about
cooking and baking and much more.'

Caramelised Nuts For Bush Sundowners

In a large heavy frying pan,
melt 30ml butter. Toss in 125ml soft
brown sugar, a generous 'fingertip load' of
sea salt, a good dash of cayenne pepper and
some finely chopped fresh rosemary.
Toss well over heat and add a heaped cup
of raw almonds or cashews.
Fry until nuts are coated in a
salty-sugary glaze.

Delicious with martinis!

10ml brown sugar

5 fresh mint leaves – shredded

2ml freshly grated orange rind

2 eggs – separated

10ml caster sugar

small knob of butter

30ml crème fraiche

50g dark chocolate – shaved

Chocolate Pan Soufflé with Orange and Mint

✳ Mix brown sugar, mint leaves and orange rind. Set aside
✳ Whisk egg yolks and caster sugar together
✳ In a separate bowl, whisk the egg whites until they form soft peaks and gently fold into the yolk mix
✳ Melt the butter in a small cast-iron pan
✳ Pour in the egg mixture and cook for 2 minutes until the underneath is just set
✳ Very carefully flip the omelette with a palette knife and cook the second side for a minute
✳ Drop the crème fraiche on top of the omelette and then fold in half
✳ Slide on to a plate and dust generously with brown sugar mix and chocolate shavings
✳ Serve hot

Serves 1

&BEYOND
Phinda Private Game Reserve

**Phinda Mountain Lodge, Phinda Rock Lodge, Phinda Forest Lodge,
Phinda Vlei Lodge, Phinda Zuka Lodge, Phinda Getty House**

Dynamic international model in wise land stewardship and wildlife conservation – an ambitious land restoration and wildlife restocking exercise saw 23 000 hectares of land restored
to pristine wilderness

✳

Six exceptional, individualised lodges

✳

Zesty-fresh food with Zulu touches for a hot climate

✳

Bush breakfasts and romantic bush dinners are daily events

✳

Winner of some of the world's most respected conservation awards

✳

Proximity to the Indian Ocean offers a memorable wildlife and marine experience

✳

Seven distinctly different habitats supporting the Big Five and an abundance of
other animals and birds

4 potatoes – peeled and cut

into 1cm dice

olive oil

1 onion – finely diced

10 eggs

250ml cream

salt and ground black pepper

1 bunch asparagus – sliced lengthways

and blanched for 1 minute

150g soft goat's cheese

Frittata of Asparagus and Goat's Cheese

* Blanch diced potatoes till nearly cooked, drain well and sauté in a frying pan in 100ml olive oil till soft in middle and lightly coloured
* Add the onion to potatoes and cook for 5 minutes
* Place eggs and cream in a bowl and beat together with a fork. Season with salt and pepper
* Add the hot potatoes, onion and frying oil to this egg mixture and mix gently
* Place frying pan back on heat and add 50ml olive oil
* Pour in the egg and potato mixture, then lower heat to a very low temperature
* Once a skin has formed on the bottom of the pan, gently 'pull' the omelette away from the edge of the pan with a spatula to allow egg mixture to reach the bottom of the pan
* Place the asparagus and crumbled goat's cheese on the frittata
* Cook until eggs are nearly set. Place under hot grill for 2 minutes to warm asparagus and melt cheese

To serve:
* Slide frittata out of pan and onto serving dish (or serve in pan)
* Frittatas are best served just warm, so allow to rest a little before serving
* Delicious with a tomato and basil leaf salad

Serves 8

Dukkah Spice Blend

250g hazelnuts
125g dried chickpeas
50g coriander seeds
50g cumin seeds
75g sesame seeds
100g salt
10 black peppercorns, coarsely ground
30g dried mint leaves, crushed

Dukkah Spice Blend (cont.)
In a heavy pan, roast the hazelnuts
and while still hot, rub off skin.
With a large knife, chop until
almost fine. Set aside.
In the same pan, roast the chickpeas,
coriander, cumin and sesame seeds
until lightly golden.
Grind in a blender until fine.
Mix with chopped hazelnuts, add salt,
black pepper and mint leaves.
Store at room temperature -
keeps for several weeks. Makes 700g.

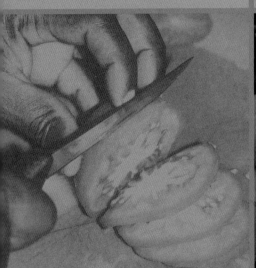

Phinda's bush breakfasts are legendary.
After an early morning start and
an exhilarating game-drive with a
stop for warm drinks, juice, muffins and
other welcome tidbits,
guests are delighted to discover that,
just when stomachs are beginning to
grumble again, they stop for an
alfresco breakfast. Hot and cold repasts
are produced as if by magic by their
ranger and tracker, and the consensus is
always that food is so much more
delicious when eaten in the
fresh morning air of the African bush.

125ml honey

125ml oil

125ml brown sugar

10ml ground nutmeg

10ml ground cinnamon

250ml sunflower seeds

500ml oats

250ml desiccated coconut

500ml digestive bran

125ml sesame seeds

125ml hazelnuts

125ml pecan nuts

125ml almonds

500g bran flakes

To serve:

honey

750ml yoghurt

500ml muesli

fresh fruit

Honeyed Muesli and Yoghurt in a Glass

＊ Heat honey, oil, brown sugar, nutmeg and cinnamon
＊ Toss the remaining ingredients together (except for the bran flakes)
   and place in a baking tray
＊ Pour over the hot honey mixture, tossing all the ingredients well
＊ Roast in an oven preheated to 180°C until golden brown, tossing regularly,
   for about 15-20 minutes. Remove from oven
＊ Finally add the bran flakes and toss one more time
＊ Store in an airtight container
＊ Serve 125ml muesli in a honey-swirled glass layered with yoghurt & fresh fruit

Serves 6

Activity before a big group event is frenetic but perfectly choreographed. Musicians tune their instruments, vocalists do voice exercises, waiters polish glasses and place gleaming cutlery on white-clad tables. Butlers, rangers and housekeepers are roped in to remove leaves from long-stemmed roses; safari vehicles disgorge a flurry of chefs in talc-white outfits; candles in candelabra are lit, a path is lined with twinkling lanterns and a vast white marquee in the middle of the bush is transformed into a magical setting for an African banquet.

Can Can Chicks

* Season chickens with salt and pepper and olive oil
* Open cans of beer, drink a mouthful of each (or toss out equivalent) and divide
  bay leaves, cinnamon, coriander, chillies and cumin between the 4 cans
* Place the cans on a baking tray and 'sit' a chicken firmly on each can
* Roast in a preheated 190°C oven for 35 minutes
* Remove from oven and rub with mustard and Dukkah Spice Blend.
  Cook for a further 25 minutes at 170°C
* Allow to rest for 10 minutes
* To serve: split chickens in half, pile on a platter and sprinkle with more
  Dukkah spice

Serves 8

4 chickens
60ml sea salt
ground black pepper
60ml olive oil
4 cans of beer – pick your favourite
4 bay leaves

4 cinnamon sticks
20ml coriander seeds
4 red chillies
20ml cumin seeds
60ml Dijon mustard
60ml Dukkah Spice Blend
(see recipe page 53)

&BEYOND
Sabi Sand Game Reserve

Dulini Lodge, Exeter River Lodge, Leadwood Lodge, Kirkman's Kamp

One of South Africa's most prestigious game reserves

✳

Renowned for unsurpassed Big Five game viewing and leopard sightings

✳

Superb South African hospitality

✳

Mouthwatering sundowner stops in memorable bush settings

✳

Delicious Pan African meals served in an African boma around a blazing campfire
under a star-strewn sky

2 large aubergines

10ml salt

1 orange

1 lemon

8 tomatoes – blanched,

skins removed and diced

1 red onion – finely chopped

4 cloves garlic – peeled and

thinly sliced

20ml sesame seeds

125ml olive oil

10ml fresh thyme leaves

125ml fresh mint leaves – shredded

Salad of Roasted Aubergine, Tomato and Mint

✱ Dice aubergines into 2cm cubes, sprinkle with salt and leave for 15 minutes
✱ Rinse briefly and dry on paper towel
✱ Squeeze orange and lemon and set aside
✱ In a bowl mix aubergines, half the tomatoes, red onion, garlic, sesame seeds, olive oil and thyme leaves
✱ Roast on a tray in a preheated 200°C oven for 25 minutes or until aubergines are thoroughly cooked
✱ Remove from the oven, place in a glass bowl and toss with remaining tomatoes, mint, orange juice and lemon juice
✱ Check for seasoning
✱ Serve either hot as a vegetable or cold as a salad

Serves 4

Three Cheese Bread and Butter Pudding

* Cut the bread into 1cm thick slices, and butter both sides
* Place these in a large, buttered ovenproof dish. Sprinkle with half the parmesan and all the cheddar
* Mix together the milk, eggs, salt, pepper and nutmeg
* Pour this mixture over the bread
* Sprinkle with remaining parmesan and finally the mozzarella
* Bake in a preheated 180°C oven for 40 minutes. The pudding will be well risen and nicely browned
* Serve immediately before pudding 'falls'
* Delicious with all roasted meats and a tossed green salad

Serves 8-10

1 day old baguette
100g soft butter
180g parmesan – grated
180g strong white cheddar – grated
1.5 litres milk

10 eggs
10ml salt
5ml ground black pepper
2 pinches ground nutmeg
200g mozzarella – grated

&BEYOND
Madikwe Safari Lodge

Three intimate camps with generously proportioned guest areas

✳

One of South Africa's largest reserves at 75 000 hectares

✳

Pan-African cuisine with a dash of quirky Groot Marico influences

✳

Evocative starlit dinners and delicious bush breakfasts

✳

Signature &BEYOND private butler service

✳

The Big Five and a rich biodiversity of mammals, endangered wild dog and 350 bird species

✳

Exclusive, malaria-free wilderness

✳

The area is imbued in history, with characters such as Mzilikazi, Dr David Livingstone,
Sir Cornwallis Harris and Herman Charles Bosman

8 mielies (corn on the cob) –
with outer leaves attached
500g sweet potato
125ml vegetable oil
2 onions – diced

15ml caraway seeds – crushed
3 jalapeno chillies –
seeded and thinly sliced
bunch fresh coriander –
washed and chopped
salt and ground black pepper

Tamales with Corn and Sweet Potato Filling

✳ Carefully peel back the outer leaves from mielies and remove from cob
  Strip kernels off husk and set aside
✳ Blanch leaves in salted water for 1 minute. Drain and refresh in iced water.
  Drain well
✳ Boil kernels in lightly salted water for 7 minutes. Strain and set aside
✳ Boil sweet potatoes till done, peel and cut into small dice
✳ In a frying pan, heat oil and sauté sweet potatoes and onions till lightly golden
✳ Add caraway seeds and cook for a further 2 minutes
✳ Finally add chillies and coriander and season to taste
✳ Divide mixture between mielie leaves. Secure each parcel with string
✳ Steam for 15 minutes
✳ Serve hot with a chilli-flavoured butter

Serves 4

White Bean Tahini

1 x 400g tin cannellini beans
45ml tahini
45ml chopped parsley
45ml fresh chopped coriander
1 clove garlic, chopped
lemon juice, salt and
ground black pepper to taste

Drain and rinse the beans.
Place in the blender with all
the other ingredients.
Blend until smooth.
Serve with deep fried
sweet potato crisps.

We were scuttling to and fro with
pots and pans, tables and chairs
and trying to hang lanterns in the
highest branches when a guttural
cough alerted us to a lioness
and her cub watching us
with great interest.
We rapidly joined the lanterns
on the highest limbs.

71

12 large lemons

1.5kg sugar

30g epsom salts

30g tartaric acid

30g citric acid

3 litres boiling water

Ouma Grietjie's Lemon Syrup

✳ Peel the rind of 4 lemons very thinly without pith
✳ Squeeze all the lemons
✳ Place rind and juice in a large bowl and add sugar, epsom salts, tartaric acid and citric acid
✳ Pour over the boiling water and stir well
✳ Leave for 48 hours
✳ Strain and pour into sterilised bottles
✳ Serve with iced water or sparkling water with fresh lemon slices and mint leaves

Makes 4 litres

&BEYOND
Kwandwe Private Game Reserve

Kwandwe Great Fish River Lodge, Kwandwe Ecca Lodge,
Kwandwe Uplands Homesteads, Kwandwe Melton Manor

Member of Relais & Châteaux whose Quality Charter subscribes to the '5 Cs':
Cuisine, Courtesy, Charm, Calm and Character

✳

Four exceptional, distinctively different lodges situated on 22 000 hectares of prime wilderness

✳

Funky Frontier farmhouse food with Xhosa characteristics

✳

30 kilometres of privately owned Great Fish River frontage. Kwandwe Great Fish River Lodge
is set along the riverbanks

✳

Widely acclaimed by the world's top travel publications

✳

Exclusive, malaria-free Big Five wilderness with both black and white rhino

✳

Extraordinary nocturnal animal viewing on extended night game drives

✳

Recognised for its sterling community development initiatives

250g cottage cheese – drained

5ml fennel seeds

1 medium red banana pepper – seeded
and cut into fine slivers

1 clove garlic – crushed

2ml coriander seeds – crushed

extra virgin olive oil

4 medium sweet potatoes

olive oil

ground black pepper

125g black olives (optional)

small bunch of coriander –
roughly chopped

Baked Sweet Potatoes with Cottage Cheese and Banana Peppers

* Mix the cottage cheese with the fennel seeds, banana pepper, garlic and coriander seeds and just enough oil to moisten. Cover and set in a cool place to allow flavours to meld
* Bake the sweet potatoes in their skins in a preheated 180°C oven
* After 45 minutes pierce with a knife to check readiness. The knife should go in easily
* When the potatoes are cooked, halve them lengthways. Brush with a little olive oil and freshly ground black pepper, and fill with the cottage cheese mixture Divide coriander between the four potatoes and serve

Serves 4

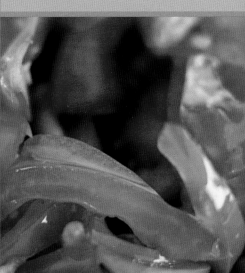

Old-Fashioned Quince Compote

Cut the quinces into fat slices. Peel and
remove pips. Add all the peel and pips to
water to cover. Boil for 30 minutes to make
a thick syrup and strain. Poach quince
slices very slowly until they turn sticky on
the outside and a deep rich red colour.
Serve chilled for breakfast with a dollop of
cinnamon-flavoured cream.

FRESH TOMATO AND FENNEL SOUP
SERVES 8
INGREDIENTS

180 ML olive oil
4 organic onions finely chopped
2 - 4 cloves organic garlic
4 organic fennel bulbs, finely chopped.
3200g Roma tomatoes roughly chopped.
about 2500 Ml tomato juice vodka to taste

Fennel to garnish

20 Ml Sugar
Salt & freshly ground black pepper

olive oil
onion garlic Fennel tomato tomato juice vodka

@ Heat the olive oil in a saucepan and lightly
fry the onions, garlic and fennel until very tender
about 10 minutes.

ⓑ Add the tomatoes & tomato juice. simmer until slightly
thickened & flavoursome, about 15 minutes.

ⓒ Strain the soup and return to a clean pan. Add
the remaining ingredients and heat through. Serve
hot or at room temperature -

ELNECK LOVERBOY MABUMDA

FRESH TOMATO AND FENNEL SOUP
SERVES 8

INGREDIENTS

180 ml olive oil

4 organic onions, finely chopped

2–4 cloves organic garlic

Fennel to garnish

Salt & freshly ground black pepper

② Add the tomatoes & tomato juice. Simmer until slightly thickened & flavoursome, about 15 minutes.

③ Strain the soup and return to a clean pan. Add the remaining ingredients and heat through. Serve hot or at room temperature.

Coffee French Toast, Vanilla Mascarpone and Grilled Peaches with White Chocolate

* In a double boiler slowly melt white chocolate. Spread onto wax paper as thinly as possible. Leave in the fridge to set
* Halve peaches and remove the stones. Place cut side upwards on baking tray.
* Sprinkle with sugar and place under heated grill until caramelised
* Split vanilla bean lengthways, scrape out all seeds and mix into the mascarpone. Set aside
* Mix together the eggs, cream, espresso and coffee liqueur. Dip the bread in this mixture
* Melt butter in a frying pan and fry bread until golden brown
* Serve bread and peaches hot with chilled mascarpone cheese and broken slivers of chocolate

Serves 4

100g white chocolate

4 ripe peaches –
blanched to remove skins

125ml sugar

1 vanilla bean

250g mascarpone cheese

3 eggs

125ml cream

100ml strong espresso

75ml coffee liqueur

4 slices white bread

100g butter

Spiced Lentils

500g brown lentils
3 onions - finely chopped
45ml olive oil
3 cloves garlic, peeled and crushed
3 cinnamon sticks
10ml aniseed
5ml each ground turmeric, coriander, ginger
15ml brown sugar
4 tomatoes - skinned and diced

Cook lentils until soft but not mushy,
set aside. Sauté the onions for
five minutes in the oil,
add the garlic and all the spices,
then sugar and tomatoes. Simmer until a
sauce is formed. Add the lentils and heat
through. Serve with poppadums.
This dish is best made the day before.

Eastern Cape Roosterkoek

400g cake flour

15ml baking powder

50ml skim milk powder

2ml salt

100g butter – cut into dice

2 eggs

150ml water

* Combine flour, baking powder, skim milk powder and salt
* Rub diced butter into dry ingredients working lightly with fingertips
* Beat eggs and water, add to dry ingredients and mix well
* Knead into a stiff elastic dough
* Shape into 6 cakes
* Grill over medium coals (or in a cast-iron ribbed pan) for 20 minutes,
  turning often

To serve:
* Split roosterkoek cakes in half while still warm, and lightly butter both halves
* Layer with grilled prosciutto, cheese and apricot preserve
* Serve immediately

Serves 6

To serve:

60ml butter – softened

6 slices prosciutto – lightly grilled

6 slices cheddar

100ml apricot preserve

Eastern Cape Roosterkoek

400g cake flour
15ml baking powder
50ml skim milk powder
2ml salt
100g butter – cut into dice
2 eggs
150ml water

* Combine flour, baking powder, skim milk powder and salt
* Rub diced butter into dry ingredients working lightly with fingertips
* Beat eggs and water, add to dry ingredients and mix well
* Knead into a stiff elastic dough
* Shape into 6 cakes
* Grill over medium coals (or in a cast-iron ribbed pan) for 20 minutes, turning often

To serve:
* Split roosterkoek cakes in half while still warm, and lightly butter both halves
* Layer with grilled prosciutto, cheese and apricot preserve
* Serve immediately

Serves 6

To serve:
60ml butter – softened
6 slices prosciutto – lightly grilled
6 slices cheddar
100ml apricot preserve

&BEYOND
Southern Africa

Victoria Falls:

Matetsi Water Lodge

Namibia:

Sossusvlei Desert Lodge

Botswana:

Nxabega Okavango Tented Camp

Sandibe Okavango Safari Lodge

Xaranna Okavango Delta Camp

Xudum Okavango Delta Lodge

Chobe Under Canvas

Savute Under Canvas

Expeditions Botswana

&BEYOND
Matetsi Water Lodges

Sumptuous riverside accommodation and private butler service

*

Zambezi riverside dining with traditional Zimbabwean hospitality

*

Only 40km from Victoria Falls village – 'the adrenaline capital'

*

15 kilometres of exclusive Zambezi River frontage

*

Diverse seasonal game-viewing with expert &BEYOND rangers

*

River activities including canoeing, riverboat cruises and tag-and-release fishing

*

Wonderful birdlife along the Zambezi riverbank

*

Large herds of buffalo and elephant, kudu, wild dog, and sable and roan antelope

3kg beef rib

10ml sea salt

1.5kg small beetroots –
washed and stalks trimmed

60ml vegetable oil

1kg baby onions or shallots – peeled

sea salt and ground black pepper

700g green beans –
blanched for 2 minutes in salted water

Roast Beef with Whole Roasted Vegetables

✳ Preheat oven to 220°C
✳ Rub the beef rib with sea salt
✳ Prepare the beetroot by boiling in salted water for 20 minutes
  Drain and set aside
✳ Place a large roasting dish over a moderate heat and add oil. When hot,
  brown the beef well on all sides
✳ Add the beetroot, cover the dish with foil and place in the oven for 10 minutes
✳ Reduce the heat to 180°C and roast for a further 15 minutes. Remove the foil
  and add the onions. Season with sea salt and freshly ground black pepper
  Return to the oven uncovered and roast for a further 30 minutes
  Finally add beans and return to the oven for 10 minutes
✳ Allow the beef to rest for 15 minutes in a warm place before carving

Serves 8

On 17 November 1855 the great missionary-explorer Dr David Livingstone was taken by dugout canoe down the Zambezi River to see Mosi-oa-tunya - 'the smoke that thunders'. Nothing could have prepared him for the sight of one of the world's greatest natural wonders - the broad, smoothly-flowing Zambezi hurtling abruptly over a precipice 1370m wide into a roaring, mist-filled chasm 108m deep.

'This is right from my heart. I am watching crocs, ellies, hippos, you name it here at the Zambezi River ... we have many opportunity ... you can do it anytime ... the chance is yours ...
Chef Elmon Dumi - Ngala

Citrus-glazed onions

1kg onions - thinly sliced
2ml salt
125ml orange juice
30ml brown sugar
pinch ground ginger
45ml butter - melted

Cook the onions in boiling salted water until just soft. Drain and place in a bowl. Blend the remaining ingredients and pour over onions. Toss well. Place in a buttered baking dish. Bake at 200°C for 15 minutes.

2 cloves garlic – peeled

500ml fresh basil leaves

30ml grated parmesan

50g macadamia nuts

2ml salt

150ml extra virgin olive oil

400g tin red kidney beans

400g tin butter beans

150g fava beans

Picnic Bean Salad with Macadamia Pesto

✳ Place garlic, basil leaves, parmesan, macadamia nuts and salt in a blender. Blend and slowly add olive oil

✳ Rinse the red kidney and butter beans well and drain

✳ Blanch fava beans in boiling salted water until just soft. Drain

✳ Toss all the beans in the pesto, check seasoning and allow to stand at room temperature for 1 hour before serving

Serves 4

&BEYOND
Sossusvlei Desert Lodge

Set in the 180 000-hectare privately owned NamibRand Nature Reserve

✳

Sumptuous yet simply presented Sossusvlei food

✳

Dune dining, picnics and sundowners

✳

Stargazing in observatory with highly sophisticated telescope – a cigars, stars and cognac experience

✳

Thrilling excursions to Sossusvlei – orange-hued and the world's highest dunes

✳

Desert-adapted wildlife thrives, including oryx, springbok, aardwolf, ostrich, hyena, bat-eared fox,
Cape fox and the endemic Hartmann's mountain zebra

✳

Desert surrounds, scenic drives and guided walks in the area exclusive to Sossusvlei Desert Lodge guests

350g smoked springbok – thinly sliced

1 bunch green asparagus – blanched

400g tin cannellini beans

1 head fennel – thinly sliced

100g fresh rocket leaves – washed

1 ripe avocado – peeled and
cut into large dice

1 orange – zest only

80 ml olive oil

10ml lemon juice

125ml basil leaves – shredded

15ml white wine vinegar

salt and ground black pepper

Smoked Springbok Carpaccio with Summer Greens

✳ Arrange the carpaccio evenly over 4 large plates
✳ Halve the blanched asparagus lengthways
✳ Rinse the cannellini beans and drain well
✳ Toss the asparagus, cannellini beans, fennel, rocket, avocado, orange zest,
   olive oil, lemon juice, basil and vinegar together. Season with salt and pepper
✳ Pile salad on top of springbok and add more basil leaves on top if you wish
✳ Note: Springbok may be substituted with smoked ostrich, smoked beef,
   Parma ham or even smoked salmon

Serves 4

The Namib is a world of immense solitude, of endless horizons, and dramatic desertscapes - hauntingly beautiful, and the world's oldest desert. From the air it is a vista of undulating sands and immense dunes, salt pans and relics of rivers that failed to reach the ocean. Underground streams' secret courses are revealed by a mantle of green amid the fiery colours of the ancient sands.

New lodge, new kitchen, new staff, new everything. The kitchen team was bristling with the eager anticipation of the first-day trainee. I was explaining how a kitchen worked when an unexpected order for a 'simple salad' came from the dining room, followed by 'Make it quick!' I turned to one trainee and asked for a cucumber ... his face told me he had no idea what that was.

I explained that it's the long green vegetable in the fridge, then realised he had no idea what a fridge was. I explained that it's the large glass box in the corner. I heard a noise and turned to see the trainees buckling under the weight ... they were bringing me the whole fridge.

For the Syrup:

600g white sugar

500ml water

30ml instant coffee granules

75ml coffee liqueur

For the Cake:

500g butter - softened

500ml brown sugar

4 eggs

20ml instant coffee granules

4 x 250ml cake flour

10ml baking powder

15ml bicarbonate of soda

15ml salt

500ml sour cream

250ml walnuts - chopped

For the Topping:

400g tub mascarpone cheese

150g walnuts – chopped and toasted

Coffee and Walnut Cake

To make the Syrup:

✳ Boil the sugar and water until a thick syrup is formed.
  Remove from the heat, add the coffee granules and liqueur. Cool
✳ Butter and flour a large chiffon cake tin

To make the Cake:

✳ Cream together the butter and sugar until light and fluffy. Add the eggs one
  at a time, beating between additions
✳ Dissolve the coffee granules in 20ml water and add to mixture
✳ Sieve together cake flour, baking powder, bicarbonate of soda and salt
✳ Fold in half the flour mixture until just mixed, followed by 250ml of the sour
  cream, then the remaining flour and finally the remaining sour cream
✳ Stir in the chopped walnuts and pour the mixture into the cake tin
✳ Bake in a preheated 180°C oven for 1 – 1½ hours or until a skewer
  comes out clean
✳ Allow to cool in the tin for 20 minutes before turning out onto a cake rack
✳ Prick all over with a skewer and drizzle over half the coffee liqueur syrup

To make the Topping:

✳ To finish, top the cake with the mascarpone and roasted walnuts
  Serve with remaining coffee liqueur syrup

Orange Pistachio Pastries

* Peel and segment the oranges. Cut the rind of 2 oranges into thick slices, remove pith and blanch the rind for 2 minutes in boiling water. Drain and set aside
* Soak the oranges in the Amaretto for at least 6 hours
* Drain the oranges and set aside. Reserve liquid for later use
* In a medium-size bowl, mix the pistachios, cinnamon, nutmeg, cardamom and ginger
* Bring the orange juice, sugar and water to a boil in a medium-size saucepan
* Reduce the heat and simmer for 15 minutes or until the syrup thickens
* Remove from the heat, add the nut and spice mixture, orange segments, orange rind and reserved Amaretto. Leave to stand at room temperature
* Prepare the pastry by rolling it out to a 2mm thickness. Cut into 5cm squares
* In a deep frying pan, heat the oil. Fry the pastry squares until crisp and light golden in colour. Drain on absorbent paper
* Dip the pastries into the syrup, pile them into a dish and pour over the syrup, orange segments and nuts
* Leave at room temperature for at least 2 hours and scatter with shredded fresh mint leaves (optional)

Serves 6-8

80ml Amaretto liqueur
250ml pistachios - shelled
2ml ground cinnamon
2ml ground nutmeg
2ml ground cardamom
2ml ground ginger

500ml orange juice - strained
250ml white sugar
250ml water
400g frozen puff pastry – thawed
oil for deep frying
125ml fresh mint leaves –
shredded (optional)

&BEYOND
Nxabega Okavango Tented Camp and
Sandibe Okavango Safari Lodge

Situated near permanent channels of the Okavango Delta (the world's largest inland delta),
ensuring a year-round water and wilderness experience

✳

Exceptional tented accommodation

✳

Delta dining at its best, with the finest and freshest of ingredients

✳

Exhilarating mekoro (canoe) or powerboat trips through the crystal-clear channels

✳

The excitement of viewing big game on land through game-drives and bush walks

✳

Architecture and infrastructure follow the principle of a light footprint in an ecologically sensitive environment

✳

Exclusive access to six broad habitats allows private sightings of a diverse array of animal, bird and plant species

&BEYOND
Xudum Okavango Delta Lodge and Xaranna Okavango Delta Camp

Each exquisite lodge is situated within its own exclusive 25 000 hectare wildlife concession

✱

Xudum and Xaranna have been designed to complement each other harmoniously. Xaranna, which takes its inspiration from the iconic Delta water lily, is decorated with soft lily pink, stone and olive green. Xudum on the other hand, is dramatically angular in design, decorated in tones of chocolate and ebony.

✱

Witness the Delta's wildlife and birdlife from the vantage point of a
traditional mokoro (dugout canoe) or game drive vehicle

✱

Exhilarating helicopter safaris offer an unforgettable bird's eye view of the Okavango Delta

✱

Memorable bush breakfasts and sundowners in beautiful, remote locations

4 fully ripened bananas

150g pecan or walnuts – roasted

250ml thick cream

2ml ground cinnamon

Roasted Bananas over the Fire

✳ Roast the bananas in their skin over coals

✳ When skins have blackened, split each banana open and sprinkle with nuts, cream and cinnamon

✳ The bananas can also be served with homemade chocolate sauce, hot fudge sauce, caramel sauce or lemon curd

Lemon Curd

4 lemons

5 eggs

250g butter – softened

400g sugar

✳ Wash lemons and grate rind very finely. Squeeze lemons and strain juice

In a glass bowl, beat eggs, then add rind, juice, butter and sugar. Place the bowl over a pot of simmering water and stir until mixture is glossy and thick enough to coat the back of a spoon

Pour into sterilised glass jars and refrigerate

&BEYOND
Chobe Under Canvas and Savute Under Canvas

A wildlife enthusiast's dream, Chobe National Park is one of the top wilderness reserves in the world

✳

Home to the largest single concentration of elephant

✳

Savute is famous for the annual zebra migration

✳

Where nature meets luxury – just six luxurious ensuite safari tents complete
with butler service amid the untamed African wilderness

✳

Delicious home-baked meals and traditional bush dinners served under the stars

Hot Spiced Orange Tea

1 litre boiling water
80ml sugar
10 whole cloves
2 cinnamon sticks
4 tea bags Ceylon Tea
one orange - juice and zest
30ml fresh lemon juice
1 lemon - sliced
80ml rum

In a saucepan, combine boiling water,
sugar, cloves and cinnamon sticks.
Bring to the boil. Add the teabags,
remove from heat and steep for
4 minutes. Add orange juice
and zest, lemon juice, lemon slices
and rum. Reheat but do not boil.
Strain, and serve in
warmed glasses.

Serves 4

For the Brittle:

400g white sugar

300ml cold water

15ml liquid glucose

5ml cream of tartar

200g mixed nuts –

chopped and roasted

For the Plums:

12 ripe purple plums –

halved and stoned 250ml sugar

30ml peeled and

finely sliced fresh root ginger

15ml butter

For the Cinnamon Cream:

10ml ground cinnamon

250ml double cream

sugar to taste (optional)

Hot Ginger Plums with Nut Brittle and Cinnamon Cream

To make the brittle:

* Place the sugar, water, glucose and cream of tartar in a large
saucepan, bring slowly to the boil stirring occasionally. Once boiling do not
stir again
* Cook on a high heat till the colour changes to a golden brown caramel
* Remove from heat. Swirl the nuts into the syrup by shaking the pan –
not stirring – and pour on to a well-oiled tray
* Allow to cool before breaking into shards
* Store in an airtight container until required (keeps for 2 days)

To make the plums:

* Mix together the plums, sugar, ginger and butter and place in a roasting dish
* Roast in a preheated 220°C oven till the syrup bubbles and thickens, and
the skins on the plums start to split

To make the cinnamon cream:

* Add cinnamon to the cream and whip till the cream forms stiff peaks
Sweeten with sugar if you wish

* Arrange the hot plums, with their syrup in a bowl
* Add a generous dollop of cream and then sprinkle over the nut brittle

Serves 4-6

Roasted nut oil

800ml cashew nuts
500ml light olive oil

Dry roast the nuts in a heavy pan.
Warm the olive oil over a gentle heat
and add the hot nuts. Remove from
the heat and cool. Store in elegant
bottles. Delicious with salads, grilled
fish and steamed vegetables

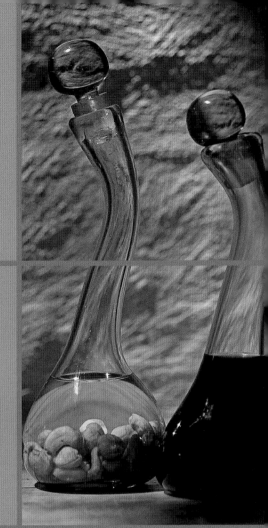

Its 5:00am - the crack of dawn has
just spilled its first rays of sunlight
onto the Delta grass, turning it into a
pale sesame-seed gold, and fine-
tuning the palm trees on the horizon
from night into light. I am in my bed
and the comforting sounds of the
askari gathering all the lanterns on
the paths to the rooms heralds the
welcoming arrival of my butler
bringing tea to my suite.
Another day in Africa begins.

&BEYOND
Expeditions Botswana

Fully serviced wilderness camping through some of the biggest and most remote game sanctuaries in Southern Africa

✳

Intimate groups of just six guests guarantee each a window seat for excellent wildlife and
photographic opportunities

✳

Luxury mobile safaris travelling to the ultimate wilderness highspots Botswana and Victoria Falls,
led by professional &BEYOND guides

✳

Lip-smackingly hearty 'bush luxe' cooking

✳

Exclusive wilderness campsites in breathtaking scenic settings

✳

Fully serviced: camp staff erect and break camp, and do all the cooking and hosting to silver service standard

✳

Opportunity for intimate wildlife and landscape observation, with specialist interests such as birding easily accommodated

500ml beer

125ml olive oil

4 cloves garlic – crushed

10ml paprika

1 red onion – finely chopped

2 sprigs rosemary

4 x 225g fillet steaks

8 small bell peppers – whole

10ml coriander seeds – crushed

salt and pepper

olive oil

2 green apples – peeled,

cored and quartered

30ml fresh rosemary – chopped

Botswana Beef and Roasted Peppers

* In a deep ceramic dish combine the beer, olive oil, garlic, paprika, red onion and rosemary
* Add the steaks and coat well with marinade. Leave for at least 12 hours
* Heat a large cast-iron pan
* Add the red peppers, coriander, salt, pepper and oil and cook over a high heat until the peppers are coloured on all sides
* Remove the steaks from the marinade and season with salt and pepper
* After the peppers have been cooking for 7-8 minutes, keeping the heat up high, add the steaks
* Seal for 3 minutes on one side and turn over
* Add the apples and chopped rosemary
* Continue cooking till steaks are to your liking and apples lightly browned

Serves 4

Chicken Sandwiches Two Ways

Old-Fashioned Curried Chicken Mayonnaise Sandwiches

✳ Toss the chicken in the mayonnaise, curry powder, chutney and spring onions
✳ Season with salt
✳ Spread the bread of your choice with a little more mayonnaise and layer
   chicken mixture with tomato slices and cos lettuce

Serves 2

Grilled Chicken & Caramelised Onion Sandwiches

✳ Gently sauté the onions in 15ml olive oil for at least 20 minutes until soft
✳ Add the brown sugar and balsamic vinegar and cook for a further 10 minutes
✳ Soak the raisins in hot water until plump. Drain and add to onions
✳ Coat chicken breasts in remaining olive oil and season with salt and pepper
✳ Grill in a hot cast-iron pan for 3 minutes on each side or until cooked
✳ Split ciabatta rolls and spread one side with mayonnaise and the
   other side with pesto
✳ Layer chicken, caramelised onions, tomatoes and rocket leaves

Serves 2

250ml cooked chicken – diced
125ml good mayonnaise
15ml curry powder
15ml fruit chutney
2 spring onions – finely chopped
salt
4 slices bread of your choice
2 roma tomatoes – sliced
cos lettuce
2 onions – thickly sliced
30ml olive oil

30ml soft brown sugar
15ml balsamic vinegar
60ml raisins
2 chicken breasts –
slightly flattened
salt and ground black pepper
2 ciabatta rolls
15ml good mayonnaise
10ml pesto
2 roma tomatoes – sliced
rocket leaves

It was very, very early.
I was setting up a bush breakfast,
everything was damp and that wet earth
and soggy grass smell overwhelming.
I looked up from where I was cooking
sausages over the fire ...
the leopard stared straight at me.
I had no rifle, nothing but a frying pan,
some eggs, sausages and champagne.
It was the sound of the cork flying from
the bottle that saved me ... otherwise the
leopard would have had hot frying pan
griddle marks across its face.

Camping bread

750ml bread flour
5 ml salt
5 ml ground cumin
15ml baking powder
2ml bicarbonate of soda
1 x 340ml can of beer
1 egg - beaten
5ml rock salt

Sift together the flour, salt, cumin,
baking powder and bicarbonate of soda.
Pour in beer and knead to form a stiff
dough. Place in a greased loaf tin.
Brush with beaten egg and sprinkle
with rock salt. Bake in a
preheated oven at 160°C for 1 hour.
Turn out and cool.
Delicious with apricot preserve
and mature cheddar cheese.

Pear and Almond Tart

For the pastry:

125g cake flour

pinch of salt

100g unsalted butter – softened

2 egg yolks

40g icing sugar

60g ground almonds

For the filling:

30ml Triple Sec

55g Italian amaretti biscuits

3 pears

80g caster sugar

2 eggs – beaten

175ml double cream

icing sugar for dusting

To make the pastry:

✳ To make the pastry, sift the flour and salt into a bowl and form a well in the centre

✳ Mash the butter with a fork

✳ Place the butter, yolks, icing sugar and almonds into the well. Quickly and lightly blend with fingertips until the ingredients just begin to come together

✳ Sprinkle a little flour over the mixture, and draw all the ingredients together by chopping through them with a cold knife

✳ When the mixture resembles breadcrumbs, draw it into a ball with fingertips Knead gently for a minute

✳ Form into a ball, wrap in cling film and refrigerate for 30 minutes before rolling out

✳ Butter a 20cm pie dish. On a lightly floured surface, roll out the pastry and use to line the dish. Prick the base of the pastry case, cover and refrigerate for 30 minutes

✳ Preheat the oven to 190°C and place a baking sheet in the oven

✳ Line the pastry with greaseproof paper and fill with dried beans

✳ Place the dish on the baking sheet and bake the pastry blind for 10 minutes Remove the paper and beans. Return to the pastry case to the oven for a further 5 minutes. Cool

To make the filling:

✳ To make the filling, sprinkle Triple Sec over the amaretti biscuits in a small bowl and leave to soak

✳ Peel, halve and core the pears. Place in a saucepan and just cover with boiling water. Add the sugar and poach for 10 minutes until tender

✳ Transfer the pears to absorbent kitchen paper to drain

✳ Stir the eggs and cream into the amaretti biscuits

✳ Arrange the pears, cut side down in the pastry case and spoon over the cream mixture

✳ Bake for 30 – 40 minutes 180°C until lightly set

✳ Serve the tart warm dusted with icing sugar

Serves 6

&BEYOND
East Africa

Kenya:

Kichwa Tembo Masai Mara Tented Camp

Bateleur Camp at Kichwa Tembo, Masai Mara

Tanzania:

Lake Manyara Tree Lodge, Lake Manyara National Park

Ngorongoro Crater Lodge, Ngorongoro Conservation Area

Grumeti Serengeti Tented Camp, Serengeti National Park

Klein's Camp, Serengeti National Park

Serengeti Under Canvas, Serengeti National Park

Mnemba Island Lodge, Zanzibar

&BEYOND
Kichwa Tembo Masai Mara Tented Camp and Bateleur Camp

Set directly in the path of the annual Great Migration of millions of herbivores

*

Romantic bush dinners on the banks of the Mara River – scene of the Great Migration crossing

*

Memorable meals in the Masai Mara served by your personal butler

*

Dew-fresh vegetables and aromatic herbs straight from the camp's *shamba* (vegetable garden) to the chef's chopping board

*

Legendary Mara River crocodile, huge herds of elephant, black-maned Mara lion, cheetah,
red-tailed monkey, Masai giraffe and much more

*

Private concession leased from Maasai landlords allows for exclusive game-viewing and
bush walks guided by Maasai naturalists

*

Celebrated Kenyan hospitality is ubiquitous – from gardeners to camp managers

*

The beautiful rolling plains of the Masai Mara offer some of the finest Big Five game-viewing in Africa, year-round

*

Situated at the base of the Oloololo Escarpment just below the spot where *Out Of Africa*'s most famous scene was filmed

250g watermelon chunks

2 pears

80ml fresh lime juice

(from 5 or 6 limes)

2ml chilli powder

2ml salt

5ml peeled and grated

fresh root ginger

100g pecorino cheese

60ml green pumpkin seeds

500ml rocket leaves –

washed and dried

Summer Salad of Watermelon, Pears and Pecorino

✳ Cut the watermelon into small cubes

✳ Peel, halve and core the pears, then quarter

✳ In a small bowl, combine the lime juice, chilli, salt and ginger and stir well to make the dressing

✳ Cube the pecorino

✳ Lightly toast the pumpkin seeds in a hot dry frying pan, about 3–5 minutes

✳ To serve, divide the rocket leaves evenly among 4 salad plates

Add the watermelon, pears and dressing. Add the pecorino and sprinkle over the seeds. Serve chilled

Serves 4

Our heads were reeling under the weight of all this newfound knowledge. Deep-fried arrowroot chips, roasted groundnuts, Jungo beans, mandaazi (similar to a doughnut) and traditional Kenyan curries were a whole new taste sensation.

Late into the dark African night we sit around the fire, mesmerised by the exotic figures of the dancing Maasai, their tall silhouettes rhythmically bobbing up and down, the reflection of the firelight on their beads adding golden flashes to their skin.

The aroma of Kenyan coffee beans roasting over the fire blends with the heavy scent of wild jasmine, wrapping itself around us like a bold Maasai blanket.

30ml mayonnaise

4 slices bread of your choice

1 small bunch watercress

2 roma tomatoes – sliced

8 wafer-thin slices of pastrami or

gammon

10ml Dijon mustard

2 dill pickles – thinly sliced

2 pita breads

250ml cos lettuce – finely shredded

30ml tahini

1 avocado – peeled and diced

1 roma tomato – diced

$\frac{1}{2}$ red onion – thinly sliced

100g roasted red peppers –

cut into strips

8 green olives – halved and pitted

100g feta – crumbled

Great Safari Lunch Sandwiches

Pastrami or Gammon Mustard Mayonnaise

✳ Spread the mayonnaise on the bread

✳ Layer as follows: watercress, tomato, pastrami or gammon, mustard and
  dill pickles

Serves 2

Vegetarian Club Pita

✳ Split the pita open to form a pocket

✳ Toss the cos lettuce with the tahini and stuff into pita

✳ Gently combine the avocado, tomato, red onion, red peppers, olives and
  feta cheese

✳ Fill pockets until brimming over

Serves 2

&BEYOND

Lake Manyara Tree Lodge

The only Lodge in small yet very diverse Lake Manyara National Park

✳

Boma dining – using ingenious cooking methods – does not get better than this!
Lake Manyara Tree Lodge is also known for its iced cocktails and delicious cocktail snacks
Superb sundowners and lakeshore picnics

✳

10 gorgeous treehouses, cradled in the boughs of mahogany trees, and beautiful elevated guest areas
provide a stunning base from which to enjoy the Park

✳

The flamingo-flanked soda lake with the towering backdrop of the Great Rift Valley makes for a spectacular landscape

✳

Remote location of the Lodge in the southern section of the Park ensures near-exclusivity of game-drives

✳

The Park is renowned for its tree-climbing lions and great herds of elephant

✳

Good birdwatching with more than 400 species

To prepare the following drinks,
blend ingredients thoroughly
Freeze into a thick slush
Serve in well-frosted glasses

Keep sugar syrup handy for
making cocktails
To make sugar syrup,
boil together equal parts of
white sugar and water. Stir to
combine and cook over a
gentle heat until syrup thickens

Frozen Sundowners

GIN & TONIC
150ml Gin
400ml tonic water
juice of two limes
500ml crushed ice

GREEN APPLE CHARTREUSE
100ml Green Chartreuse
400ml apple juice
juice of 1 lemon
30ml sugar syrup
500ml crushed ice

SWEET BOURBON
150ml Bourbon whiskey
150ml sugar syrup
juice of 4 lemons
750ml crushed ice

LIME BITTERS
juice of 4 limes
10ml Angostura Bitters
10ml sugar syrup
50ml grenadine
500ml crushed ice

GASPER PETER

PRAWNS ON THE PLATE

KEY

———————→ PRAWNS

———————→ PARSLY

———————→ PARSLY CHOPED

A trainee chef and I were on duty that
night. All the other chefs had the night
off - after all, it was merely a private
dinner for the Honourable Minister and
the Director ... and the bodyguards
arrived and arrived and arrived.
I realised that the 911 section of the fridge
(reserved for emergencies) was going to
take severe strain.

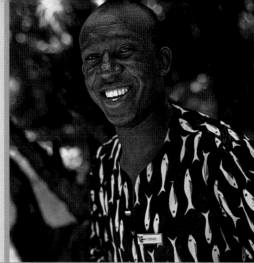

During the second Food Workshop
we stressed the 'how' (ie the importance
of the way we do things) to impress
upon the chefs that we may not
have the fancy ingredients that Europe
and America have but our total
package is even more important.
Later when asked what is the most
important part of a meal,
Sidilion from Lake Manyara
Tree Lodge answered 'I learned that
I am the magic ingredient
in every meal'.

911 Green Gazpacho

Blend all green ingredients
in fridge, eg:
Avocado
Celery
Cucumber
Parsley
Green apple
Spring onions

Blend with apple juice,
a touch of olive oil and
a pinch of green chilli.
Season with salt to taste.

147

1.5kg chicken pieces
2 onions – quartered with
skin left on
2 carrots – roughly chopped
3 litres water
5cm knob fresh root ginger
3 sticks lemon grass – bruised
2 red chillies
2 bunches coriander – washed
2 cloves garlic – crushed
1kg noodles (rice, egg, sorba or pasta)
15ml sesame oil

2 bunches coriander –
washed and stalks removed
8 kaffir lime leaves
3 green chillies – seeded and
finely sliced
15ml finely sliced fresh root ginger
500ml bean sprouts
500g Portabello mushrooms –
sliced
125ml finely sliced spring onions
juice of 2 lemons
sea salt to taste

Laksa of Mushrooms and Chillies

* Combine the chicken, onions and carrots in a roasting dish and roast for about
  40 minutes in a preheated 180°C oven
* In a large saucepan, combine the water with the ginger, lemon grass, chillies,
  coriander and garlic
* Remove the chicken from the oven, discard onions and carrots and add to
  the rest of the ingredients in the pot
* Simmer for about 40 minutes. Strain and return the stock to the stove. Bring to the boil
* Cook the noodles in the boiling stock
* Heat the sesame oil in a frying pan and toss in the coriander leaves, lime leaves,
  chillies, ginger, bean sprouts, mushrooms and spring onions. Stir-fry for 5 minutes
* Once the noodles are cooked, add the mushroom mixture to the soup, season with
  lemon juice and salt to taste, heat through and serve

Serves 8

We had a simple menu that night under the stars – the trees bedecked with lanterns, the fire tossing crackles into the air and the Maasai appearing and disappearing into the darkness around us ... Fillet of Kenyan Beef with an African Hollandaise. Fresh Mangoes drenched with Vanilla Anglaise. It all went wrong when a herd of wildebeest came rushing past for no apparent reason – we ran for cover and the hollandaise and the anglaise bowls were swopped in the melee ... funny, but no-one said a word!

Spiced oranges

5kg oranges
225ml white wine vinegar
500g sugar
5ml whole cloves
4 cinnamon sticks

Cut the oranges into wedges. Place in a pot with water to cover. Simmer partially covered for 1 hour until the peel is tender. Boil the vinegar, sugar and spices for 5 minutes. Drain the oranges but reserve the cooking liquid. Place half the oranges in the vinegar / sugar syrup and simmer for 30 minutes, covered. Drain and repeat with the remaining oranges, adding cooking liquid if necessary. Cool and leave overnight. Next day, reboil syrup until thick. Place the oranges and syrup in sterilised jars.

&BEYOND
Ngorongoro Crater Lodge

On the rim of the Ngorongoro Crater – one of the Seven Wonders of the World and a World Heritage Site

✳

'Maasai meets Versailles' on the tables of this exceptional lodge

✳

Dramatic picnics are enjoyed during game-drives on the floor of Ngorongoro Crater

✳

Private butler service includes romantic private dinners at the fireside in your suite

✳

Extraordinary, award-winning architecture with magnificent Crater views

✳

Interpretive game-drives into the Crater are led by professional &BEYOND guides

✳

Fresh roses adorn each spectacular suite, with its romantic chandelier-lit slipper bath and rich furnishings

✳

Ngorongoro Crater is the permanent home of up to 25 000 animals

✳

Excursions to the world-famous Olduvai Gorge, a cultural Maasai village, Lake Nyasa and Lake Ndutu are available

2 pieces of star anise
2 whole cloves
1 cinnamon stick
15ml rock salt
2ml caraway seeds
2ml grated lemon zest
10ml white sugar
4 x 170g duck breasts –
skin scored
30ml butter

200g kumquats – quartered
2 onions – roughly chopped
3 red chillies – seeded and
roughly sliced
10ml grated fresh root ginger
5ml whole allspice
5ml salt
1 apple – peeled and grated
2 peaches – stoned and diced
500ml sugar
500ml white wine vinegar

Duck with Kumquat and Chilli Marmalade

✳ Grind the star anise, cloves, cinnamon, rock salt, caraway seeds, lemon zest
and sugar to a fine powder
✳ Season the duck with the spice mixture and allow to rest for 20 minutes
✳ In a medium-size frying pan, sauté the duck in butter for 8–10 minutes
✳ Allow to rest for 5 minutes before slicing thickly
✳ Serve with Kumquat and Chilli Marmalade

Serves 4

Kumquat and Chilli Marmalade

✳ Blanch the kumquats for 30 seconds in boiling water. Drain
✳ In a heavy pot, simmer the kumquats, onions, chillies, ginger, allspice, salt,
apple, peaches, sugar and vinegar for 1 hour or till thickened and quite soft
✳ Cool, store in sterilised jars and refrigerate

1 litre cream

2 litres milk

15 egg yolks

700g caster sugar

12 fully ripened bananas

100ml white rum

Banana and Rum Ice-Cream

✳ Bring the cream and milk to the boil

✳ Whisk together the egg yolks and sugar until light and fluffy

✳ Slowly add the hot milk/cream to the eggs. Mix well and return to the pan

✳ Cook very gently, until slightly thickened. Remove from the heat and strain the custard into a clean bowl

✳ Blend the banana and rum until smooth

✳ Stir into the cooked custard

✳ Freeze in an ice-cream machine according to manufacturer's instructions

Serves 12

The grandeur of the
Ngorongoro Crater elevates every
wedding to the sublime.
The transcendent views,
thick carpets of rose petals strewn as
far as the eye can see, traditionally
attired Maasai choirs,
a personal butler for every
wedding guest, wondrous
bridal banquets …
a truly unforgettable start to a
charmed honeymoon

Halva Rosewater Ice-cream

5 eggs
125g caster sugar
20ml rosewater
750ml cream
250g halva - grated

Whisk the eggs, sugar and
rosewater together until very thick and
fluffy. In a separate bowl, whisk
the cream until soft peaks
are formed. Fold in the halva.
Fold cream and halva mixture into
eggs/sugar mixture. Freeze.

Serves 4

"The only thing we were unhappy about is
how much weight we were gaining! We ate
so much delicious food and it was never-
ending! The chefs really added a lot of
unique style and flavour to each meal, so
it was inevitable that we ate absolutely
everything that was presented to us, with
much delight!"

Lodge Guest Book

Lobster

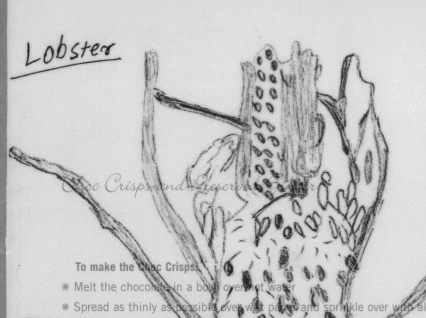

Choc Crisps and Preserved Ginger

To make the Choc Crisps:
* Melt the chocolate in a bowl over hot water
* Spread as thinly as possible over wax paper and sprinkle over with almonds
* Allow to set in a cool place
* Break into desired sizes

To make the Preserved Ginger:
* Blanch the ginger for 2–3 minutes in boiling water and drain
* Place the ginger and sugar in a large saucepan and cover generously with water (4–5 litres)
* Bring to the boil then turn down heat to a very, very slow simmer. Cook until ginger is softened and syrup has thickened. This must be done slowly and over a period of 10 hours or more. Keep topping up with water as necessary
* Store in a sterilised jar and refrigerate
* Serve with choc crisps, espresso and a shot of Grappa

By BRIGHTON

For the Choc Crisps:
200g dark chocolate
150g nibbed almonds – toasted

For the Preserved Ginger:
500g fresh root ginger –
peeled and sliced into 2mm slices
700g sugar

161

&BEYOND
Grumeti Serengeti Tented Camp

Grumeti lies in the path of the Great Migration, with the Grumeti River and its gigantic crocodiles one of the most dramatic crossings of this natural phenomenon

✳

A flamboyant, wittily designed camp, Grumeti offers a colourful complement to the magnificent Serengeti plains

✳

Novel Grumeti River-side dining, with 'en suite' hippos! All meals are prepared on traditional 'jikos' (fires) and in stone ovens

✳

Dramatic sundowners on the Masira Hills are accompanied by delicious, inventive snacks

&BEYOND
Klein's Camp

Bordered to the north by the Masai Mara and to the west by the Serengeti, Klein's Camp is situated on the return path of the Great Migration

✳

Sizzling Serengeti cuisine with a hint of wildness served overlooking the Kuka Hills

✳

Bush dinners in the hills overlooking the verdant valleys are breathtaking, with lanterns adorning tall trees, and damask-clad tables sparkling with silver, crystal and candlelight

✳

A vegetable *shamba* (garden) supplies the lodge chefs with fresh, enticing vegetables and herbs to enhance their culinary creations

For the Muffins:

250ml cake flour

10ml baking powder

2ml salt

5ml ground cinnamon

125ml wholewheat flour

80ml granola

60ml dark brown sugar

1 egg – lightly beaten

125ml unsalted butter – melted

125ml milk

5ml grated lemon zest

80ml raspberry preserve

80ml smooth cottage cheese –
optional

For the Glaze:

60ml brown sugar

60ml granola

2ml ground cinnamon

30ml unsalted butter – melted

Granola Muffins with Raspberry Preserve

To make the Muffins:

* Lightly grease a muffin tin and preheat the oven to 180°C
* Sift the cake flour, baking powder, salt and cinnamon
  Add the wholewheat flour, granola and sugar and combine
* Make a well in the centre
* Place egg, melted butter, milk and lemon zest in the well. Stir with a wooden spoonuntil ingredients are combined
* Fill one third of each muffin mould. Spoon 5ml raspberry preserve (and 5 ml cottage cheese if so desired) into each one. Top with remaining muffin mix

To make the Glaze:

* Combine the sugar, granola and cinnamon with the melted butter and gently spoon over the muffins
* Bake for 20–25 minutes until nicely browned and firm

Makes 12 Muffins

Klein's Camp joined forces with Tanzania's Njiro Wildlife Research Centre to train 10 Maasai women in the art of bee-keeping. The project was met with great excitement and there was much good-natured competition for a place in the daily training sessions. 'Fortunately', says the project manager, the bees played along and colonised the hives quickly.

The first harvest was a scene of joyous celebration. Today, the Maasai honey is sold in Klein's Camp's curio shop, and the proceeds are used to buy more of the traditional log hives, bottles and labels involved in its production. Profits are also allocated towards training more women in this age-old Maasai tradition.

Roasted Nut Honey

60ml almonds
60ml pine nuts
60ml macadamia nuts
180ml strong wild honey

Dry roast the nuts in a heavy pan until rich gold in colour. Warm the honey over a gentle heat and toss in the hot nuts. Store in sterilised jars. Delicious with ice-cream, greek yoghurt or roasted bananas.

4 bulbs fennel – halved

20ml olive oil

salt and

ground black pepper

30ml butter –

at room temperature

250ml white sugar

4 ripe pears

30ml tarragon vinegar

400g puff pastry

Tarte Tatin of Roasted Fennel and Pear

* Coat the fennel with olive oil, salt and pepper
* Place on an oven tray with 125ml water and cover with tin foil
* Bake in a preheated 150°C oven for 35–45 minutes or until tender
* Rub a 28cm ovenproof frying pan with the butter. Sprinkle over all the sugar
* Cut the pears in quarters and remove core. Lay these alternately with the roasted fennel bulbs, cut side down, on the sugar. Season with a little salt and pepper
* Save the juices from roasting the fennel and add it to the vinegar for later use
* Roll out the puff pastry to generously cover the frying pan. Prick the pastry all over with a table fork. Lay over the fennel and pears
* Place frying pan on stove and start to cook. Watch carefully as the sugar will start to caramelise – you are looking for a golden caramel, not too dark
* Place back in oven and cook for 25 minutes or until pastry is golden and crisp
* Remove from the oven and invert onto a serving plate
* Return the pan to stove and deglaze using vinegar and reserved fennel juices
* Pour this over the tart and serve piping hot

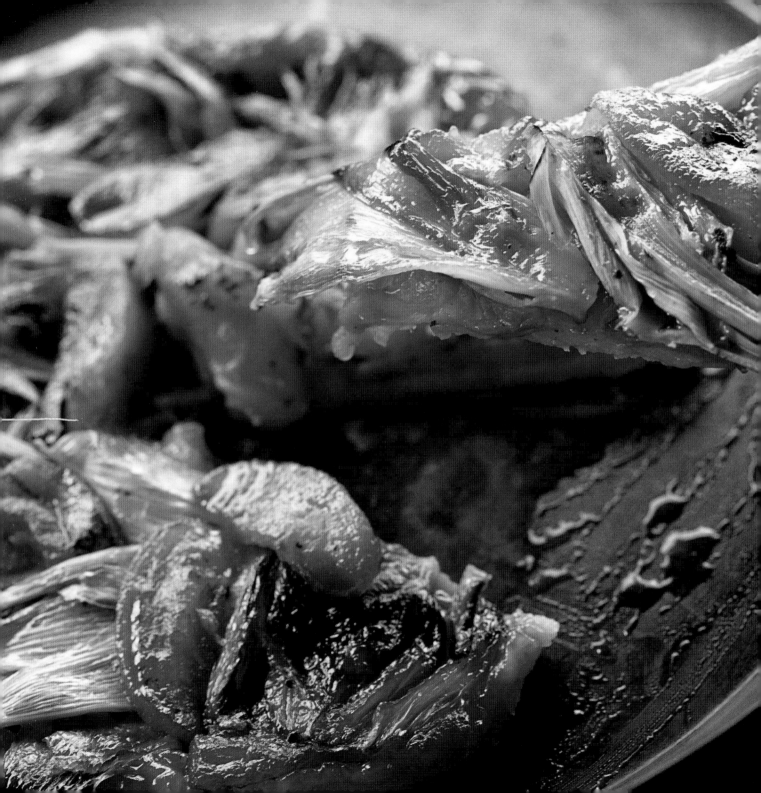

Safari Kitchen Magic

A great tuna lay over the coals.
It was stuffed with fresh herbs from the
shamba and brushed with olive oil and
lemon. The aromas it offered up drew a
number of pre-dinner visits to the fire.
Chef Richard stood proudly behind his
contribution to the main course as it
attracted compliments.
One peckish guest asked him,
'So Richard, from where do you get your
fish out here in the middle of nowhere?'

He was no doubt expecting a romantic
answer about old fishermen, in their
dhows, trawling off the African coast
and then dispatching their catches up an
ancient wagon trail to arrive in camp just
in time for dinner.
Instead, Richard looked at him smiling
and said "As if by magic…"
James Hendry

200g parmesan – grated

15ml cake flour

15ml semolina

1 egg

15ml rock salt

10ml whole black mustard seeds

15ml olive oil

12 ice cubes

4 tots vodka

2 tots gin

half tot dry vermouth

6 crisp Granny Smith apples

Parmesan and Black Mustard Seed Wafers

✳ Mix all the ingredients together to form a thick paste
✳ On a greased or non-stick baking tray, use your fingers to spread the mixture out thinly into desired shape
✳ Bake at 170°C till wafers are golden brown
✳ Cool on a rack and store in an airtight container

Green Apple Martinis

For this you will need a fruit juicer/extractor. Bought apple juice can be used, but it's not really the same

✳ In the container of your juicer that collects the juice from the fruit, place the ice, gin, vodka and dry vermouth.
✳ Cut the apples into pieces suitable to be chopped by your machine
✳ Extract juice from apple and colour from skin
✳ Shake well with other ingredients and serve

Whole Roasted Baby Chickens With Green Olives

2ml saffron threads
60ml hot water
10ml ground cumin
10ml paprika
5ml ground black pepper
5ml ground coriander
4 x 500g baby chickens
125ml olive oil
15ml salt

* Soak the saffron threads in the hot water and allow to stand for about 5 minutes. Strain and reserve the water
* Mix the saffron threads with cumin, paprika, black pepper and coriander
* Rub the baby chickens with the olive oil and salt – both inside and out and then rub with spice mix
* Place in a preheated 180°C oven for 45 minutes. Check by pricking the thigh to see if the juices run clear
* Remove from oven, place on clean tray and allow to rest
* In the roasting pan in which chickens were cooked, fry the onion until lightly browned
* Add the lemon juice, reserved saffron water, ginger and any juices that have seeped from the cooked chickens, together with fresh coriander and olives
Heat through and serve with the chicken

Serves 4

1 onion – finely chopped
2 lemons – juice only
15ml finely chopped
fresh root ginger
1 bunch coriander –
washed and chopped
500ml green olives –
stones removed

Culinary observations by a Game Ranger:
"Apart from unparalleled wildlife experiences, days at &BEYOND Lodges are filled with a number of unique gastronomic events. To start off the day, there is the early morning rusk. This first provision is the most peculiar. The development of the rusk lies somewhere in the annals of settler history. There was simply no time to bake fresh cakes and scones. One had ox wagons to fashion, veldskoens (bush shoes) to mend, cattle to water and game to shoot. There were also battles to wage against imperialist red coats threatening from the south and hordes of marauding savages perceived to the north.

So it was that this easily prepared stale slab of sweet bread with the odd raisin thrown in became an African culinary highlight. Many a morning have I chuckled to myself as a guest, not from these parts, picks one of these biscuits up and attempts to bite into it. The effect is rather like watching someone try to sink his teeth into an iron rod. It is then that the confused traveller looks around for instruction. He observes a ranger dunking one of the baked bricks into his coffee, instantly rendering it the perfect morning snack".

Scott's Pineapple Chutney

8 large onions - chopped
100ml vegetable oil
45ml cumin seeds
8 green chillies - roughly chopped
8 cloves garlic - crushed
2kg brown sugar
2.5 litres white vinegar
4 cinnamon sticks
6 pineapples - peeled & diced

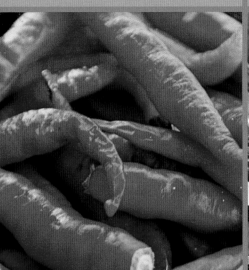

In a very large pot, gently fry onions with
oil, cumin seeds & garlic.
Add brown sugar, vinegar and cinnamon
and bring to the boil.
Add chillies & pineapple and allow to
simmer for about 1 hour.
Blend half the mixture and
return to the pot.
Cook for a further 30 minutes, till
thickened and glossy,
Store in sterilised glass jars
Serve with roasted meats.

&BEYOND
Serengeti Under Canvas

These sumptuous, elegant tented camps move around the Serengeti year round,
bringing guests within range of the world-famous Great Migration

✳

The locations of these migratory camps are carefully plotted to coincide with the documented movements
of the vast herds of wildebeest and zebra

✳

Memorable sundowners and picnics amid the thundering hooves

✳

Where nature meets luxury – just six luxurious ensuite safari tents complete
with butler service and surrounded by the untamed African wilderness

✳

Delicious home-baked meals and traditional bush dinners served under the stars

Prune and Venison Pan Pie

100ml vegetable oil

3kg venison (or beef) – cubed

2 onions – diced

2 litres veal stock (or water)

4 carrots – diced

1 head table celery – thickly sliced

15ml black peppercorns

4 bay leaves

10 juniper berries

1 bouquet garni

250g prunes – halved and pitted

250ml port

250g pancetta – cubed

2 onions – diced

4 cloves garlic – thinly sliced

ground black pepper

500g frozen puff pastry –
defrosted

15ml milk

✳ Heat the oil in a heavy casserole and brown the venison well on all sides.
Remove from the pot

✳ Add a little more oil, if necessary, and saute the onions for 10 minutes
Add the veal stock, carrots, celery, peppercorns, bay leaves, juniper berries and
bouquet garni. Add the browned venison

✳ Cover the casserole and bake in a preheated 150°C oven for at least 3 hours
until the meat is meltingly tender

✳ Strain the meat and other ingredients from the stock and return the stock to the
stove. Boil briskly until reduced to approximately 2 cups. Place the meat back
into the reduced stock and keep warm

✳ Soak the prunes in the port and set aside

✳ In a hot frying pan, sauté the pancetta cubes for 5 minutes until lightly browned
Add the onions and fry for a further 5 minutes. Add the garlic and season with
freshly ground black pepper. Add the prune and port mixture and bring to the boil

✳ Combine the venison and prune mixture in a cast-iron pan or pie dish,
checking the seasoning

✳ Cover with pastry (prepared according to instructions) and brush with milk

✳ Bake in a preheated 180°C oven for 25–30 minutes or until cooked
and golden brown

Serves 8

&BEYOND
Mnemba Island Lodge

Mnemba Island is a true barefoot island paradise, like a jade in the setting of the aquamarine Indian Ocean,
just off mainland Zanzibar

✳

Seafood any fresher would still be swimming! Fruits of the ocean are presented mezze style and in
various innovative dishes. Fresh fruit such as coconuts, bananas, limes and mangoes are purchased daily
from the market in Zanzibar, as are the exotic spices – Zanzibar is justifiably called the 'Spice Island'
and produces an array of fragrant spices including its famous cloves

✳

Just ten cottages on an otherwise uninhabited island overlook the endless beaches and dhow-bedecked waters

✳

Safe swimming in balmy waters, spectacular diving and snorkelling in gorgeous coral reefs, gentle
sea breezes and pristine white beaches are the stuff of holiday dreams

✳

Activities are varied, including swimming, walking, snorkelling, windsurfing, kayaking, fly-fishing,
deep-sea fishing and scuba diving. Alternatively, one could simply relax on the shaded beach loungers or
languish in the open-sided guest areas with a good book

✳

On Mnemba's 'house reef' alone, approximatley 274 species of fish have been recorded

30ml olive oil

15ml sesame oil

5ml chilli oil

2 shallots – peeled and finely diced

2 cloves garlic – peeled and crushed

30ml fresh coriander stems – chopped

5cm piece fresh root ginger – peeled and grated

1 red chilli – seeded and diced

375ml dry white wine

2 bay leaves

2 strips dried orange peel

500g crab claws

1kg mussels – cleaned

600ml water

2ml saffron threads

500g fresh fish – cubed

8 spring onions – washed and sliced

12 cherry tomatoes – peeled

salt and ground black pepper

Zanzibar Fish Soup

* Heat the three oils in a large saucepan
* Add the shallots, garlic, coriander stems, ginger and chilli and cook until soft but not brown
* Add the white wine, bay leaves and orange peel and bring to the boil.
* Simmer for 10 minutes and add the crab
* Cover the pan and cook for 5 minutes. Add the mussels and cook for a further 5 minutes until the shells open. Discard any mussels which stay closed. Remove the mussels and crab claws and set aside
* Pass the cooking liquid through a fine sieve. Add water and saffron
* Bring the fish broth to a simmer and add the fish cubes. Cook for 2 minutes, then add the spring onions and cook for a further 2 minutes
* Add the cherry tomatoes, mussels and crab claws and cook until heated through Season to taste with salt and black pepper
* Serve with lightly spiced cooked brown rice, sorghum wheat or millet if desired

Serves 4-6

Spiced Orange Ice-cream

30ml green cardamom pods
3 oranges – juice and zest
2ml ground cinnamon
250ml full-cream milk

* Place the cardamom pods in a mortar and pestle, mash until all the pods have opened, then remove the green pods and mash the black seeds further
* Place the orange juice and zest in a small saucepan and simmer gently until reduced by half. Cool, then chill
* Place the cardamom seeds, cinnamon, milk and cream in a pan, scald and set aside to cool and infuse for at least 30 minutes
* Beat the egg yolks until creamy. Reheat cream mixture, whisk 10ml into the egg mixture, then beat in the remaining cream, little by little
* Stir in the sugar, transfer to a double boiler, and cook, stirring, until the mixture coats the back of a spoon. Do not allow to boil, or the mixture will curdle
* Remove from the heat, dip the pan into cold water to stop the cooking process, then cool and chill. When well chilled, stir the orange mixture and custard together, strain, then churn and freeze
* Serve with Fig and Orange Cigars (see recipe page 187)

Serves 4

250ml whipping cream
4 egg yolks
100g caster sugar

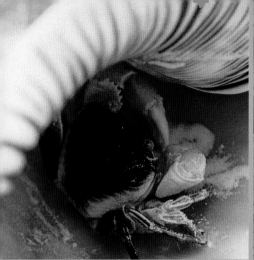

'This is what inspired me when creating some of the dishes in Mnemba Island's repertoire: sitting in a dhow on an aquamarine sea, surrounded by bursting beetroot, lusty limes, baskets full of fresh tamarind, zatari (wild thyme), vanilla pods, fiery red saffron, bunches of fragrant lemon grass, fresh banana flowers, plantains, heaps of ginger and fresh mint – all of which I'd found in the Zanzibar market.'

Rouille

Liquidise 2 red peppers, skinned and chopped, 4 small red chillies or 20ml chilli paste with 4 cloves of crushed garlic, 30ml soft breadcrumbs and 2ml salt. Keep the blender running and trickle in 100ml olive oil as if making mayonnaise. Store in an airtight container in the fridge.

Espressotinis

* Mix all ingredients together
* Sweeten well with sugar
* Freeze into a thick slush
* Serve in frozen glasses

Serves 2
Delicious served with mascarpone-stuffed dates studded with almonds and preserved ginger

1 double espresso
90ml vodka
30ml dry martini
sugar to taste

Fig and Orange Cigars

* For the filling: gently fold figs, cream, honey and orange zest together. Chill
* For the biscuits: in a saucepan melt together sugar, syrup, butter and orange juice
* Remove from heat and stir in the flour
* Place a large teaspoonful of biscuit mix on greased baking sheet and bake in a preheated 170°C oven
* Once golden brown allow to cool until firm enough to handle
* Roll around the handle of a large wooden spoon. Slide off and repeat process. Allow biscuits to cool
* Just before serving fill with fig mixture
* Serve with Spiced Orange Ice-Cream (see recipe page 183)

Makes about 30 biscuit cigars

150g fresh figs – chopped
250ml cream – lightly whipped
30ml honey
1 orange – zest only
150g sugar
125g golden syrup
100g soft butter
1 orange – juice only
125g cake flour – sifted

Behind the Scenes at a Bush Dinner

Richard, the chef, set his large fillet down by the fire and moved off to finish his red wine reduction. As he turned his back, a hyena shot out from the shadows of the mopane tree and, without missing a stride, grabbed the freshly marinated fillet and hurtled off into the woodland. Richard stared dumbstruck as the main meal disappeared into the vastness of the African night. Gretha, the hostess, threw another cocktail down the hatch. Clifford the barman returned presently from a mercy mission to fetch cocktail glasses which had been left behind at the lodge. He waved cheerfully on approach and then applied the brakes, which failed. He continued past, grinning toothily, until met head on by a large mopane tree. Steam billowed from beneath the hood as the driver emerged, still smiling and sporting a fresh forehead wound. He carried with him the miraculously unscathed cocktail glasses. There was no main course and Shadrak, the head waiter, who was double-checking the table settings, found a full table of eight place-settings to be wanting. He informed Gretha. She checked her watch, looked at the mangled wreckage of the Land Rover, at the bleeding but still beaming Clifford and then chugged the fresh cocktail she was mixing. Thus fortified, she instructed Clifford to sit down somewhere far away from any guests when they arrived and told the bristling side burns and dark glasses of Timot, the tractor driver, (despite the sun having set an hour previously) to commandeer the tractor and head back to the lodge with careful haste to fetch a fillet, a table and eight chairs. Timot chugged off towards Venus glimmering in the western sky. He arrived back just as the first game-drive spotlight was seen flickering in the night sky in the distance, Clifford, who had fashioned himself a makeshift bandage from an elastic band and some mopane leaves, was dragged from the comfort of his recovery spot. All helped to unload the remaining vital equipment. The game-drive vehicle was in sight, the guests' excited voices audible in the still night air. Shadrak was loaded with table and chairs. As the table hit the ground a cloth was thrown over it. Nathaniel flung cutlery into place, Geoffrey placed glasses.

Chairs were arranged. The new fillet was tossed eight metres across the clearing into the arms of the waiting Richard who placed it deftly onto the fire. Clifford, who now resembled Shakespeare's Puck, was dispatched to his out-of-sight recovery spot. Fresh cocktails were thrown into the well-used shaker and hurriedly poured into the glasses. Garnish could not be found as Richard had inexplicably used it on the fillet now satiating a hyena clan not far away. Gretha hastily tore some leaves off a guarri tree and presented herself neatly just as Hendrik, the ranger pulled up with eight cheerful guests. 'Welcome to bush dinner,' said Gretha, smiling and proffering drinks. *Thud!* Norman, the waiter, plummeted from a tree in which he was hanging the last lantern. The guests seemed not to notice, probably due to the oral shock of the mind-numbing cocktails. One by one the game-drives arrived. The numerous lanterns looked as if the stars had fallen gently to earth and been caught up in the trees. The smell of roasting meat and potatoes filled the still night air as the moon rose over the scene, bathing it in a warm dim light. Cheerful laughter rose to the star-emblazoned skies as cocktails were quaffed and stories shared.

Thank You!!!

To our guests – thank you for coming to Africa and affording us the opportunity of feeding you.

To Nicky Fitzgerald, mastermind and mentor, inspirer, motivator, hospitality and service guru and valued friend. None of this would have happened without you.

To Steve Fitzgerald, much admired leader of us all, who understands us all, who stands behind us all and is desperate for us to GROW UP!

To Scott, fabulous friend, awesome chef and teacher of great cooks-to-be and cookies far and wide across Africa.

To Shona, who writes, edits and generally turns the ordinary word into the extraordinary.

To Dook, divine to work with, awesome photographer and passionate cook!

To &BEYOND's Lodge Managers and Staff – who deliver it all with passion and pride, day in and day out.

To Dumi, with whom I worked at Londolozi for a very long and very happy time.

To Debra Fox and Jacqui Hunter who inspire, cajole, support and kick my butt, and try to keep me focused.

To Chris Browne who creates inspired interiors to cook by ...

To my family who just love, watch and wait

To my mother, who ignited the passion for hospitality in the beginning.

To Liz and Murray who monitored and mentored all the way.

To Cate Davies whose great patience and passion brings out the magic in all those whom she trains.

And

To &BEYOND - the most awesome company and family of extraordinary people in the world.

To our publisher Linda de Villiers, who was brave enough to tackle this labour of love.

THANK YOU!!!

Metric Conversion Chart

VOLUME AND LIQUID MEASURES

1 litre	4 cups
750ml	3 cups
500ml	2 cups
375ml	$1\frac{1}{2}$ cups
250ml	1 cup
125ml	$\frac{1}{2}$ cup
80ml	$\frac{1}{3}$ cup
60ml	$\frac{1}{4}$ cup
45ml	3 tablespoons
30ml	2 tablespoons
20ml	4 teaspoons
15ml	1 tablespoons
10ml	2 teaspoons
5ml	1 teaspoon
2ml	$\frac{1}{2}$ teaspoon

WEIGHTS

900 g	2lbs
450 g	1lb
270 g	9oz
180 g	6oz
90 g	3oz
60 g	2oz
30 g	1oz

OVEN TEMPERATURES

Deg C	Deg F	Gas
100	200	1
120	250	1
140	275	2
160	325	2
180	350	3
200	400	4
220	450	5-6

Acknowledgements

Grateful thanks to: *House and Leisure* magazine, Sumien Brink and Annemarie Meintjes from *Visi* magazine and *Taste* magazine; To our valued &BEYOND guest Christian Sperka for wildlife photographs; John Warbuton-Lee; and to &BEYOND rangers for general wildlife photographs; and Dook www.dookphoto.com. Copyright c/o &BEYOND

Index